ROUGH GUIDES WALKS & TOURS
MALLORCA

YOUR TAILOR-MADE TRIP
STARTS HERE

Tailor-made trips and unique adventures crafted by local experts

Rough Guides has been inspiring travellers with lively and thought-provoking guidebooks for more than 35 years. Now we're linking you up with selected local experts to craft your dream trip. They will put together your perfect itinerary and book it at local rates.

Don't follow the crowd – find your own path.

HOW ROUGHGUIDES.COM/TRIPS WORKS

STEP 1

Pick your dream destination, tell us what you want and submit an enquiry.

STEP 2

Fill in a short form to tell your local expert about your dream trip and preferences.

STEP 3

Our local expert will craft your tailor-made itinerary. You'll be able to tweak and refine it until you're completely satisfied.

STEP 4

Book online with ease, pack your bags and enjoy the trip! Our local expert will be on hand 24/7 while you're on the road.

BENEFITS OF PLANNING AND BOOKING AT ROUGHGUIDES.COM/TRIPS

PLAN YOUR ADVENTURE WITH LOCAL EXPERTS

Rough Guides' English-speaking local experts are hand-picked, based on their experience in the travel industry and their impeccable standards of customer service.

SAVE TIME AND GET ACCESS TO LOCAL KNOWLEDGE

When a local expert plans your trip, you save time and money when you book, even during high season. You won't be charged for using a credit card either.

MAKE TRAVEL A BREEZE: BOOK WITH PEACE OF MIND

Enjoy stress-free travel when you use Rough Guides' secure online booking platform. All bookings come with a money-back guarantee.

WHAT DO OTHER TRAVELLERS THINK ABOUT ROUGH GUIDES TRIPS?

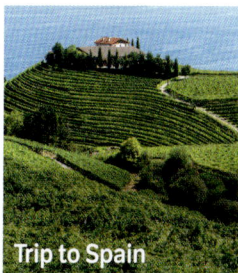

Trip to Spain

This Spain tour company did a fantastic job to make our dream trip perfect. We gave them our travel budget, told them where we would like to go, and they did all of the planning. Our drivers and tour guides were always on time and very knowledgable. The hotel accommodations were better than we would have found on our own. Only one time did we end up in a location that we had not intended to be in. We called the 24 hour phone number, and they immediately fixed the situation.

Don A, USA ★★★★★

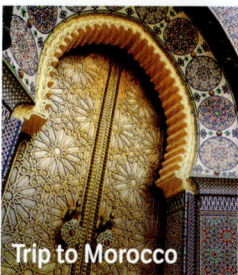

Trip to Morocco

Our trip was fantastic! Transportation, accommodations, guides – all were well chosen! The hotels were well situated, well appointed and had helpful, friendly staff. All of the guides we had were very knowledgeable, patient, and flexible with our varied interests in the different sites. We particularly enjoyed the side trip to Tangier! Well done! The itinerary you arranged for us allowed maximum coverage of the country with time in each city for seeing the important places.

Sharon, USA ★★★★★

PLAN AND BOOK YOUR TRIP AT ROUGHGUIDES.COM/TRIPS

CONTENTS

Introduction

Trip plans

Directory

Art collections

Discover the wonders of Palma's top three art galleries (walk 2), admire the extraordinary collection at a small-town train station (walk 7), or marvel at the artistic interpretation of local wine labels (tour 14).

Best walks & tours for...

Family adventures

Take an alternative approach to kids' theme parks and head instead for Mallorca's extensive network of caves and grottoes (tour 11), or kick back with a bucket and spade on the longest beach in the south (tour 12).

Foodies

Shop for edible treasures at Palma's atmospheric delis and sweet shops (walk 3), or pack a picnic of treats from local markets (tour 13).

The great outdoors

Snorkel the uninhabited island of Sa Dragonera off the southwest coast (tour 4) and enjoy the slowed-down pace of Pollença life (tour 8).

Historical legacy

Soak up Palma's Arabic provenance and old Jewish quarter (walk 1), admire the ancient monasteries and sanctuaries of Mallorca's hinterland (tour 13), or bag yourself a slice of old-fashioned mountain life (tour 5).

Literary genius

Discover the Mallorca of George Sand and Robert Graves (tour 6), or find out how light and landscape equals poetry at the Cap de Formentor (tour 8).

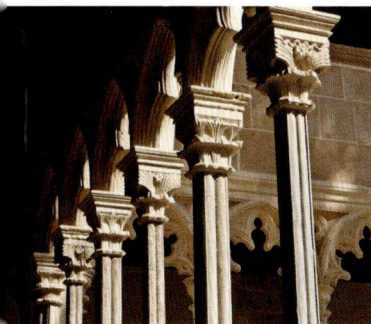

Mallorcan architecture

Explore the ancient heart of Palma (walk 1), or be dazzled by the extravagant decor of Sóller's Modernista mansions (walk 7).

Surf, sand and sun

Escape the crowds at some of the island's most hidden beaches (tour 10), or join the cool kids on the strands of the south (tour 12).

INTRODUCTION

An introduction to Mallorca and what makes it special, what not to miss and what to do when you're there.

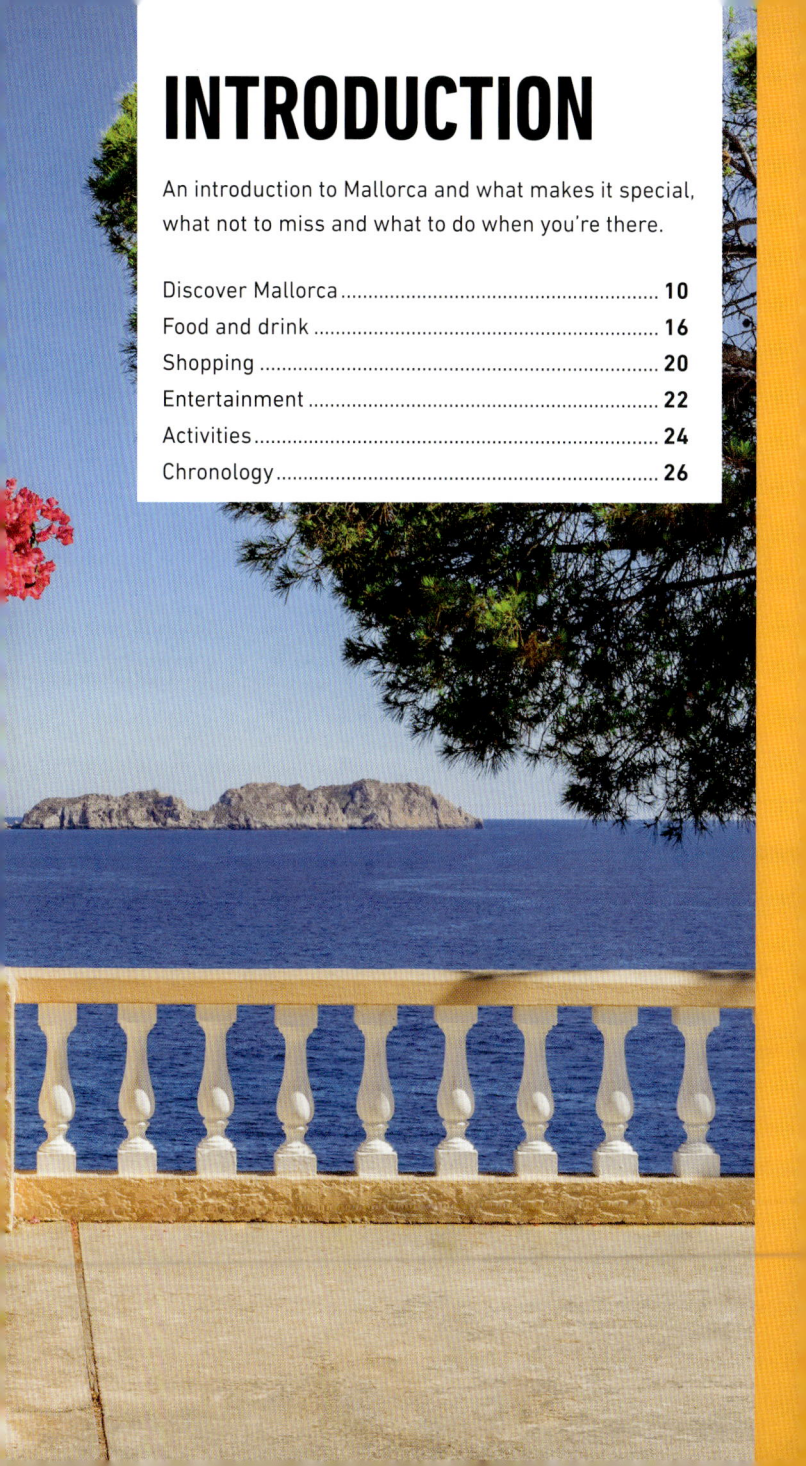

Discover Mallorca

Often spoken of as the 'pearl of the Mediterranean', Mallorca lures with sun, sand and sea, but also has plenty of other charms to recommend it, from a cosmopolitan capital to a stunning interior made for active exploration.

Palma has more than enough to offer for an entertaining long weekend, but it's the 'other Mallorca', the road less travelled, that keeps people coming back for more. Whether you're looking for secluded sands or hip clubs to dance the night away in, remote country villages or soaring mountain tops, five-star golf courses or pristine diving in crystal-clear waters, the biggest of the Balearic Islands has something to suit everyone.

Geography and layout

The Balearic Islands were formed nearly 100 million years ago when limestone bedrock was forced upwards, creating a peninsula jutting out to sea from the present-day Spanish coast around Valencia. Mallorca is the biggest of the four main islands – Menorca, Ibiza and Formentera are the other three – and offers travellers a diverse landscape: long, sandy beaches and isolated rocky coves are framed by sapphire-blue seas and backed by dramatic mountain peaks, while olive groves and vineyards fringe the sparsely inhabited interior. Not for nothing is the island often referred to as the Spanish mainland in miniature. Mallorca may be the largest

of the Balearic Islands, but it is not a big place. It has more than 550km of coastline, but at its widest point – Cap de Sa Mola in the southwest to Capdepera in the northeast – it is only 100km across; at its narrowest, from the Badia d'Alcúdia in the north to the Badia de Palma in the south, it is just half that distance. Despite its small size, Mallorca offers a variety of experiences.

Getting around

Mallorca makes for easy travelling, and the walks and tours in this guide have been arranged to run clockwise around the rim of the island, starting in Palma and ending up in the centre. It is by no means exhaustive – there is still plenty to explore on your own – and hiring a car is advisable. Driving on the island is easy, and with the notable exception of the MA-15, which cuts across the centre, is generally fairly trouble-free in terms of traffic.

The main cities featured are easy to walk around, Palma included, and for routes 1, 2, 3 and 7 you can easily get around on foot or by public transport. Outside the towns there is a train network with one

Village of Deià

line running from Palma to Sóller, another inland from Palma to the likes of Binissalem, Manacor and Inca; there is also an extensive bus system. However, if using public transport, you need to plan in advance and will need to allow extra time.

Walking/hiking paths around the island have been opened up and are generally clearly marked, and a number of hilltop sanctuaries provide rest and respite for walkers; natural parks are widely promoted and user-friendly.

History and architecture

Skeletal remains indicate that the Balearic Islands were inhabited from as early as 4000 BC, but the oldest architectural ruins date from the 3rd millennium BC. The Talayotic Age that followed – from 1500 BC to the Roman conquest – left the most archeological testimonies on the islands, the defensive stone structures called talayots, believed to have been built by a people who came from the eastern Mediterranean. The Carthaginians, whose occupation dated from the mid-seventh century BC, recruited Balearic mercenaries whose stone slings were the terror of the Romans. It was not until 20 years after the destruction of Carthage (146 BC) that Rome was able to subjugate the islands.

The Romans settled in Mallorca, but had little interest in the island beyond using it as a stopgap on more important missions of conquest. It was

really with the arrival of the Moors in 902 that it advanced in terms of commerce and agriculture, cuisine and culture, language and education. Later, under the Aragonese king Jaume II, the island entered a 'golden age', when some handsome little villages sprang up in rural areas such as those featured in route 5, and heaps of money were poured into gentrifying the important towns and cities.

By the fifteenth and sixteenth centuries, however, the gap between rich and poor stoked the fire of civil unrest, which was manifested in endless uprisings, while prosperous towns like Palma, Sóller and Andratx lived in constant fear of pirate attacks. Compounded by the arrival from mainland Europe of the plague, which wiped out a hefty chunk of the population, these were dark days for Mallorca.

Modernista Mallorca

By the time of the Napoleonic Wars (1799–1815) many islanders had cast in their lot and moved to the New World as the land of new opportunity. Wealth eventually came back in the form of the lavish Modernista (Catalan Art Nouveau) mansions of the island's main towns, coloured hydraulic tiles made famous by Huguet (https://huguetmallorca.com/en/), and the stained glass and whimsical wrought iron of the Belle Epoque. Travellers interested in architecture shouldn't miss

Fishing harbour of Sant Elm

walks 1 and 7, which feature some of the island's finest landmark buildings.

Boom and bust

Things were quiet throughout much of the twentieth century – even the Spanish Civil War (1936–9) didn't really reach Mallorca's shores – until, in 1960, the opening of Palma's Son Sant Joan airport to international traffic brought the first proper rush of tourists. This was in keeping with Franco's vision of turning great swathes of the Spanish coastline into tourist resorts along the lines of those he had heard about in Florida. Huge resorts like Magaluf and others along the east coast sprang up over the next 40 years, but the flow of foreign cash slowed – by the 1990s the island had managed to position itself alongside the Costa del Sol and Benidorm, with a reputation for dishing up a particularly virulent strain of mass tourism that put many people off coming.

The new Mallorca

Mallorca has never been a place to sit back and let things happen, and the early years of the twenty-first century have seen it smarten up its act considerably, in keeping with the needs of the more discerning traveller. Boutique hotels sprang up in Palma, and the tourist office stopped advertising sun, sea and sangria and started marketing *agroturismos* (smart rural hotels, often with a foodie focus), cycling holidays and a vast portfolio of cultural events. Even the budget airlines have come under fire from some tourism officials, who say they attract the 'wrong sort of tourist'. While that may be somewhat misplaced – it is not unheard of for millionaires to check in with easyJet, after all – twenty-first-century Mallorca is definitely a class act and that is exactly the way many islanders want it to stay.

Climate

Mallorca's climate is temperate most of the year, although it does get its wintry spells (even, on some occasions, snow in the high Tramuntana). November, December and January can also see many businesses on the island closed. July and August, by contrast, can get extremely hot and the hotels rammed. Generally, then, spring and autumn are the best times to visit, with balmy temperatures and fewer crowds.

Population

The population of Mallorca is just over 960,000, nearly half of whom live in Palma. Compare that to the 10 million-plus tourists the island welcomes every year and you get a sense of just how busy the island can be. A sizeable chunk of the population is made up of resident expats (mainly British, German and Scandinavian).

Local customs

Islanders, with the exception of farmers in very rural communities, are

Son Matias beach in Magaluf

Don't leave Mallorca without ....

Going underground. Mallorca's landscape is packed with stunning caves and grottoes, a feature of the porous limestone of the Balearic Islands. The Coves d'Artà are some of the most spectacular that can be visited. See page 66.

Savouring gourmet goodies. From sweet *ensaimadas* to New Mallorcan Cuisine, farmers' markets and freshly caught fish, Mallorca is a foodie's dream. See page 16.

Shopping 'til you drop. Whether you're looking for designer labels or traditional arts and crafts, Mallorca has something to offer all tastes and budgets. See page 20.

Admiring the views. The west coast has some stunning scenery and the best places to take it all in are from the viewing points Mirador de Ricard Roca and Mirador de Ses Ànimes. See page 42.

Tasting the local wines. Wine has been made on Mallorca since Roman times. Today you can visit several winemakers, both modern and traditional, to sample the local vinos. See page 80.

Lazing on a beach. Mallorca's beaches are legendary, whether you are looking for the white powdery sand of Es Trenc or lying on a sunbed at the private Puro Beach. See page 71.

Getting away from it all. Escape from the crowds with a trip through the Serra de Tramuntana, a UNESCO World Heritage Site, or book a stay in a mountain-top sanctuary. See page 44.

Visiting Deià. Famed for its potent mix of literary, artistic and celebrity heritage, Deià is a stunningly pretty village clinging to the side of a mountain. The home of Robert Graves, who wrote some of his novels here, is open to the public. See page 48.

Having a go at a watersport. From bumping over the waves on an inflatable banana to sailing, windsurfing and diving, there are watersports schools right around the island catering for all levels. See page 25 and page 62.

Appreciating the art and architecture. Explore Palma's world-class art galleries and learn about the Modernista movement at Can Prunera in Sóller. See pages 35 and 51.

bilingual, speaking both Mallorquín (a dialect of Catalan and the first language of the island) and Castilian fluently. In the main tourist areas you will find that many people also speak some English and German, and there is nearly always someone about to help should you find yourself stuck.

Do bear in mind that Mallorcan hours follow those of Spain: shops open around 10am, lunch is served from 1.30–3.30pm and dinner from

S'Hort del Rei (King's Garden), Palma

Modernista architecture

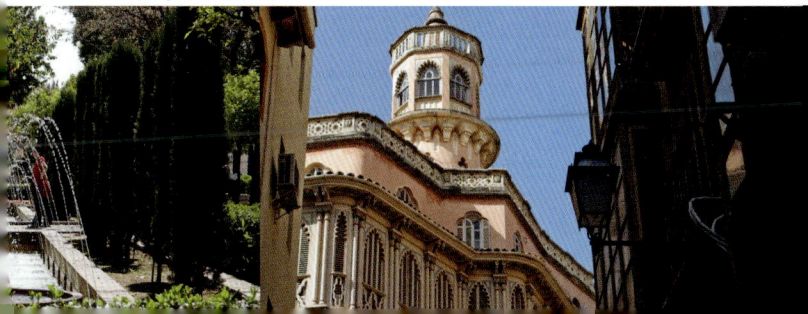

Responsible tourism

After a series of protests against over-tourism, Mallorca has emerged as one of the more contentious holiday destinations in Europe. Here are a few measures you can take to lessen your footfall:

Travel by train and bus. Mallorca possesses a good rail network that covers much of the island - and where the train doesn't go, buses do. Public transport is far better for the environment than hiring a car.

Hop on a bicycle. Much of Mallorca is flat, making cycling a feasible proposition for the vast majority of visitors. Even better, Palma's cycle lanes are well-signposted and well-maintained, whilst cycle-hire outlets are ubiquitous across the whole of the island.

Join a beach clean-up. Predictably, all sorts of rubbish gets washed up on Mallorca's beaches, but the fight back is picking up pace with, for example, the Palma Aquarium (www.palmaaquarium.com/en) organising around a dozen beach clean-up days a year.

Avoid high season. Travelling in low season (November–March) helps to reduce crowds and pressure on local resources.

9pm onwards. You can drop in for a tapa and a glass of wine in any bar at pretty much any time of day, but many places are closed on Sunday night and all day Monday. The main museums are generally open all day (although many close on Monday), but smaller ones may shut for a siesta. And out of season (November to the end of January) many places close down altogether.

Politics and economics

Something of a political conundrum, Mallorca has over 30 political parties, each of which competes for seats in both the island council – the Consell de Mallorca – and the much more powerful Balearic Parliament, which also meets in Palma; the Balearics are one of Spain's 17 autonomous regions. At the time of writing, a conservative coalition governs the Balearics led by Marga Prohens of the Partido Popular, PP (People's Party).

Tourism, and the related infrastructure, is now Mallorca's main source of income, accounting for around 80 percent of the island's GDP. More than half of all residents work in the sector, and people come from other parts of Spain as well to take up seasonal jobs. Despite its benefits, many locals remain wary of uncontrolled tourism in Mallorca, complaining of spiralling property prices and rents, the dilution of local culture and fears over long-term sustainability. The green-minded government of yesteryear responded with the introduction of a sustainable tourist tax that came into force on 1 July 2016 and it looks to remain.

Basílica de Sant Francesc, Palma

Top tips for exploring Mallorca

Menú del día. The lunchtime menu is an economical way to eat as you usually get three hearty courses with bread and a glass of wine or small bottle of water for a low price (usually €15–25).

The rebaixes. Sales in Spain are fantastic, not least because they seem to get longer each year. You'll get the cream of the crop at the start but the real bargains towards the end. Winter sales start on 7 January until 6 March and summer sales last all July and August.

All the island's a stage. Music lovers should head to Mallorca in July or August when the island becomes one long concert, especially in the towns of Deià, Pollença, Valldemossa and Artà which host world-class music festivals.

Palma's night of art. With more than 30 participating galleries and museums, Palma's Nit de l'Art gets more ambitious every year. It lasts from 7pm–midnight on the third Thursday in September. Entrance to all exhibitions is free. See www.illesbalears.travel/en/ibiza/events-la-nit-de-lart.

A quiet beach. The Cala Bóquer is an isolated beach about an hour's walk from Port de Pollença. To get there, head for the roundabout at the top of Carretera Formentor, bear left and continue uphill past the Finca Bòquer (a private house) northeast of the town centre to put you on the path of the Bóquer Valley to the beach.

Manacor's artificial pearls. Manacor may be the largest town on the east of the island and the birthplace of tennis player Raphael Nadal, but there is only one strong reason to visit and that's to invest in Mallorcan pearls. Majorica (Via Palma 7; www.majorica.com; free) offers guided tours of its facilities and cut-price jewellery.

Take a day trip to Menorca. Catch the morning ferry from Port d'Alcúdia and return on the evening one from Ciutadella. Contact Baleària (www.balearia.com) for details.

Wheelchair-friendly transport. All of Palma's buses have wheelchair access, including those that go to the airport. Several taxi companies have specially adapted taxis: try Mallorca Taxi (www.mallorcataxi.com) or Taxi Tour Mallorca (www.taxitourmallorca.com).

Reduced admission fees. Look out for vouchers in local magazines and newspapers, as well as tourist offices, which offer reduced admission fees to many attractions.

When it rains. Head inland to the Mallorca Fashion Outlet shopping centre (www.mallorcafashionoutlet.com) in Marratxí (Carretera Palma-Inca Km 7; exit 8). Here you'll find shops selling discounted clothes from previous seasons, a cinema, a bowling alley, cafés and a children's play area — perfect for a rainy day.

The hike to Cala Bóquer

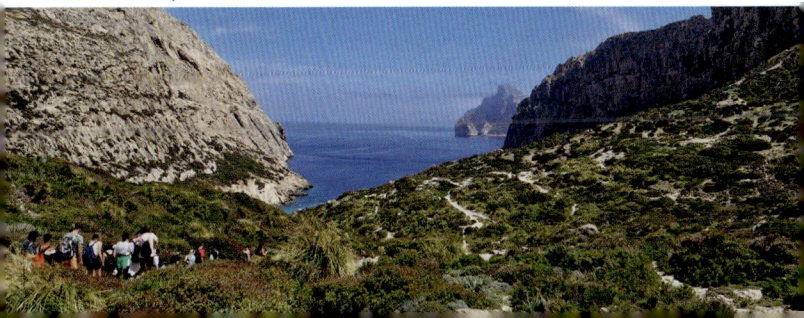

Food and drink

It took Spain a long time to realise that its larder was as well stocked and delicious as that of France, its chefs and restaurants every bit as talented. Now it has there's no stopping it, and Mallorca is no exception.

From traditional *cellers* (see page 82) and fishermen's shacks to the proponents of *Nou Cuina Mallorquina* (New Mallorcan Cuisine) – creative young chefs are serving innovative food, and not just in Palma, but all over the island. The sheer diversity of food and eating in Mallorca is thrilling, but you do need to know where to look. The restaurants section of this guide (see page 94) therefore focuses on more local places to eat, and avoids fast food and the bland, 'international-style' meals on offer in the bigger resorts. More importantly, armed with just a little background knowledge of the island's rich culinary heritage you'll be well set up for seeking out hidden treats of your own.

Local cuisine

Traditional *cuina Mallorquina* (Mallorcan cuisine) reaches its height in the old-fashioned *cellers* of the hinterland, but can be found in many other places, too. Local, humble ingredients – fruit, vegetables, pulses and grains – provide the backbone of the cooking, complemented and enhanced by locally caught fish and seafood (there are plenty of functioning fishing ports, some with excellent restaurants, dotted around the coast, as well as in Palma). Pork – particularly the native *porc negre* – appears in various guises, and island lamb, rabbit and small game birds like partridge and quail are also excellent. Increasingly, small producers of cheese, honey, chocolate and other delicacies are also emerging.

Bread two ways

In nearly every restaurant in Mallorca you will be offered *pa amb oli* (bread and oil), although these days it's ramped up a bit with a small dish of olives and one of *alioli* (garlicky mayonnaise). It's at its best when made with a dark, rustic island bread.

For breakfast you are more likely to be given *pa amb tomaqàet* – the ubiquitous Catalan snack of toasted bread rubbed with a juicy tomato and drizzled with olive oil and a sprinkle of salt. It sounds simple, but is one of the great treasures of the Catalan kitchen and not to be missed. Many hotels serve it as part of their breakfast buffet, while tapas bars do theirs topped with charcuterie, plump little anchovies or *escalivada* (a salad of roasted vegetables).

Mercat de l'Olivar, Palma

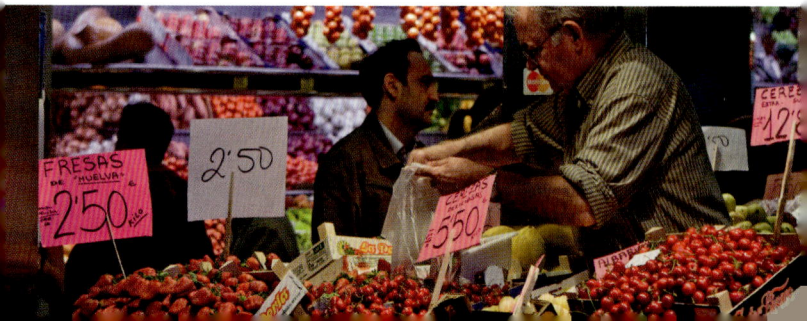

The importance of pork

For centuries, pork has been the cornerstone of the islanders' diet. Every family, no matter how poor, fattened a pig every year and, after the *matança* (slaughter), filled the larder with sausages, chops and lard, which formed the foundation of many dishes, both sweet and savoury.

At its most challenging, pork is presented in the form of *frit Mallorquí*, a platter of fried nasty bits liberally seasoned with fennel and mint. More easily digested, perhaps, are the succulent *sobrasadas* (soft pork sausage flavoured with *pimentón*), *butifarró* (coarse grilling sausages), *blanquet* and *camaiot* (cured pork sausages with varying degrees of fat and blood) that you see hanging from the rafters of restaurants and delicatessens.

Popular pork dishes are *llomb amb col* (pork rolled in cabbage leaves and baked) and *arròs brut* (rice with pork or sometimes chicken). *Lechona asada* (roast suckling pig) is really a Christmas dish, but may be found on menus at other times and has been indicated where relevant throughout the walks and tours' sections of this book.

Vegetarian delights

Unlike in much of Spain, vegetarians will do well here. The island has a rich variety of vegetables – among them aubergines, peppers, chard, crunchy lettuces, good potatoes and juicy tomatoes (including the revered *tomàtiga de Ramellet*, a vine tomato with a thick skin grown specifically for making *pa amb tomàquet*, and which you see hanging on strings in markets all over the island).

In summer, dishes such as *trempó*, a salad of tomatoes, onion and green peppers, are popular; *tumbet,* aubergines, potatoes and sweet red peppers covered in tomato sauce and beaten egg and oven-baked, is a great favourite.

Soups

Sopas mallorquinas – invariably referred to in this plural form – are ubiquitous. They are soups made of seasonal vegetables and poured over *pa pagès* (country bread sliced very thin). An interesting variety is the *sopes de matances*, which include small pieces of pork and *setas* (a type of mushroom).

Fish and seafood

Although there are as many fish dishes as there are varieties of fish, two that are especially worth trying are the *anfós al forn* (baked sea bass) and the *caldereta de peix* (spiced fish stew, a version of bouillabaisse). *Caldereta de llagosta*, a rich lobster and tomato stew laced with saffron that is a Menorcan speciality, is also popular, particularly along the north coast. Look out also for *pescado al sal* – whole fish baked in a thick shell of sea salt to preserve the flavour and juices –

A traditional spread of tapas and sangria

Food and Drink Prices

Throughout this book, the price of a two-course meal for one with a glass of house wine is represented with a price code as shown below:

€€€€ = over €45
€€€ = €30–€45
€€ = €20–€30
€ = below €20

which, surprisingly, doesn't make the fish taste too salty. Finally, if you're a seafood-lover, don't miss the sweet, pink prawns from Sóller – wildly expensive but absolutely worth it.

Cakes and pastries

Savoury pastries are found in bakeries *(panaderías)* or pastry shops *(pastelerías)*. *Empanades* are small round pies filled with meat and peas; *coca de verdura* is similar to a pizza but is rectangular in shape and eaten cold; while the *cocarois* is half-moon-shaped and filled with *bledes* (chard).

Dolç (desserts) range from the typical *gelat de ametla* served with *coca de gató* (almond ice cream with almond cake) to large, star-shaped biscuits called *crespells* and *coca de patata* (a sweet bread that is a speciality of Valldemossa), as well as *greixonera de brossat*, a type of cheesecake. The *ensaimada,* a spiral-shaped, sugar-dusted confection, is most commonly eaten with coffee at breakfast time.

Where to eat

At breakfast time you might stop at a pavement café for a cup of coffee and a pastry, then pop into a tapas bar or market stall mid-morning for a quick pick-me-up (a glass of cava or *vermut*, perhaps) and a tapa. For lunch Spanish workers head to a neighbourhood restaurant for a *menú del día* (an inexpensive set meal), then maybe have another tapa somewhere in the early evening. Dinner can be formal or consist of a *tapeo* (a tapas hop) around several bars. Naturally, the best fish restaurants are on the coast and around port areas, while the best fine dining is scattered across the island. And don't discount restaurants in the centre, which showcase some of the finest traditional cooking.

Restaurants in Mallorca cover a wide spectrum, from the excellent to the mediocre, from the local to the international. There is also an emphasis on Basque cooking, which is regarded as one of the best regional cuisines in Spain; and there are refined dishes with a French flair in the more expensive restaurants. Several top-notch chefs are working on the island and, while a meal in one of their restaurants is not cheap, it is considerably less expensive than it would be in one of the European capitals.

Drinks

Mallorca's wine industry goes from strength to strength, and you won't

Tumbet – aubergine, potato and red peppers

Food markets

If you're into food, don't miss a trawl around Mallorca's various fresh-product markets (especially if you are self-catering). Aside from the sheer bounty of produce available, it's a great way to rub shoulders with local people. Great buys include olive oil, olives, cheese, charcuterie, jams, honey and seasonal fruit and vegetables.

Tuesday morning: head for Artà, which has a wide range of foodstuffs as well as local crafts – see tour 10.

Wednesday morning: Sineu is excellent for a taste of old village life, and is one of the very few that still has a livestock section. If you're following tour 12, the afternoon market in Colònia de Sant Jordi is an atmospheric place to end the day and pick up snacks for a casual dinner on the beach.

Thursday morning: Inca's market is the largest on the island, while Lluc (tour 6) and Sant Llorenç (tour 11) also have markets on this day.

Friday morning: stop by to pick up local wines in Binissalem (tour 14) as well as tapas items to go with them.

Saturday morning: Palma has three permanent markets, but the farmers'-cum-artisan market that comes into town on Saturday is second to none.

Sunday morning: gather supplies for tour 13 in Felanitx, or for tour 6 in Valldemossa, and find somewhere to have lunch with a view.

go far wrong if you stick to locally produced wines (see tour 14, page 80). Cava (sparkling wine from Catalunya) is also popular, as is a *caña* (a small draught beer). Most of the beer hails from mainland Spain: San Miguel, Moritz and Estrella de Galica are all brands to try out. Neighbouring Ibiza's Isleña is a light, refreshing pilsner-style beer available all over the island.

Practicalities

As in the rest of Spain, people in Mallorca eat late. Lunch is generally from 1.30pm to 3.30pm and dinner from around 9pm until late. Restaurants that open their doors earlier tend to be at the touristy end of the spectrum, but this can be useful if you're travelling with children.

Tipping

Tipping is a bit of a grey area. If you want to round up to the nearest euro at the bar if you've only had a snack, that's fine, but not expected. Leaving 5 percent at lunch or dinner is acceptable, and if you are eating somewhere high end, leaving 10 percent is the honourable thing to do.

Forn des Teatre is a Palma bakery that specialises in ensaimadas

Shopping

It may not be Madrid or Barcelona, but Mallorca does have a few treats for the consummate shopaholic. Eschew designer labels in favour of island arts and crafts or gourmet products and you'll find a treasure trove of purchases to be discovered.

If Palma is a hotspot for local fashion, interiors and shoes (many of the brands are cheaper than they would be on the mainland), the rest of the island has fostered a high-class cottage industry of locally made goods. The discerning traveller can pick up beautiful textiles to translate into bed and table linen back home, classy handmade espadrilles (the rope-soled summer shoe traditional to Spain as a whole), some of the world's finest olive oil and almonds, and a host of other quirky trinkets for gifts.

Most small shops open from 10am–2pm and 5–8pm from Monday to Saturday while high-street chains generally stay open all day, sometimes until 10pm.

What to buy

Glass, pottery and ceramics

There are two glassblowing factories that can be visited: Lafiore (www. lafiore.com), at S'Esgleieta 7km from Valldemossa (see tour 6, page 46), and Vidriera Gordiola (www. gordiola.com), just before Algaida on the Palma–Manacor road. Both do a strong line in wacky, psychedelic-coloured bowls and glasses.

The village of Prtol, a short distance northeast of Palma, has the most working kilns on the island. It is also the birthplace of *siurells*, the red, white and green clay-figure whistles, said to have originated during the era of Muslim rule. Alternatively, shop for cooking pots: here are two main types: *ollas* (round) and *greixeras* (flat and shallow).

Textiles

The *roba de llengües* (cloth of tongues, pronounced 'yengos'), is named for the colourful, tongue-shaped patterns stamped onto a cotton-linen weave. It's extremely popular for home textiles – tablecloths and bed linen as well as upholstery – and can look surprisingly chic and effortlessly contemporary. Working looms clatter away at the Museu Martí Vicenç in Pollença (see tour 8), but there's a greater selection of textiles for sale at Bujosa Textiles, Carrer Bernardo Santa Eugenia 53, Santa Maria del Camí (www.bujosatextil.com; see tour 14).

Glassblowing in action

Leather and straw

Mallorca used to be renowned for the quality of its leather goods, but the industry has declined considerably. Inca is still home to the better-known brands and factory outlets. If you like shoes, then you'll love shopping in Mallorca. You can go to the factory shop of the quirky shoe company Camper (on the main road around Inca), whose highly individual shoes have become well known. The brand also has outlets in Palma, in Avinguda Jaume III and Carrer Sant Miquel. Elsewhere you will find *abarcas*, the slipper-like sandals from Menorca that have been worn by local workers for centuries and now come in a range of colours for around €35. They've become something of a cult item in recent years, the hipster alternative to the espadrille.

Food and drink

Ensaimadas (see page 18) are sold in individual or family sizes, in appropriate packages for export. Buy them in just about any bakery in Palma. Markets are the best places for olives, cheese and charcuterie, or go to an old-fashioned deli like little Colmado Santo Domingo (see walk 3). Vineyards are found around Binissalem–Consell–Santa Maria (see tour 14), and in the southeast around Felanitx, and wines are worth buying here. Mallorca is also known for its herbal liqueurs, the most popular being the aperitif Palo Tunel, made in Bunyola.

Antiques and flea markets

There are various well-known antiques shops, most notably in Santa María, Pollença and Sóller. In Palma, Antigüedades Casa Delmonte, Carrer Riera 5 (www.casadelmonte. es), Persepolis, Avinguda Jaime III, 23 (www.persepolis-antiques. com), and Midge Dalton at Plaça Mercat 20 (http://antiguedades-midge-dalton.spanishtrade.co.uk), are good but expensive, while the Baratillo (flea market), which takes over the Avinguda Gabriel Alomari Villalonga every Saturday morning, is great for bargains. Go early.

Palma's stores

Avinguda Jaime III is lined with designer and high-street stores selling fashions, jewellery and gifts. El Corte Inglés, Spain's biggest department store chain, is a good one-stop shop for national and international brands. The Passeig des Born has an interesting variety of shops, ranging from high-quality leather luggage and accessories at Loewe to the city's flagship Zara.

Fine Books, a treasure trove of second-hand English books, is at Carrer Morey 7, near Plaça Major, and there are a number of chic fashion boutiques on Carrer Verí. The Centro Porto Pi, a couple of kilometres west of the centre, is the place to go for high-street brands. Another large shopping complex includes FAN Mallorca, Calle Cardenal Rossell s/n (http://fanmallorca.com).

Colourful ceramics

Mallorca-founded shoe brand

Entertainment

Mallorca is as lively and cultured as one could hope for in a place of its size. The great Catalan artist Santiago Rusiñol said islanders 'take the moon' as others 'take the sun', so come prepared to spend long, balmy nights beneath the stars.

The most popular of all Spanish pastimes is to sit out on a plaza in the cool of the night, sipping cold *cañas* (small draught beers) and chatting the hours away. Even the smallest of village seems to burst into life the minute the sun goes down, but Mallorquíns, like all Catalans, are also great patrons of the arts, and Palma is blessed in having a city council that throws considerable funds at keeping its citizens happy. Note that much of the performance art is in Catalan or Spanish, which makes it tough going for non-speakers, though there's plenty else to enjoy that doesn't depend on knowing the language.

Theatre and film

Theatrical performances and classical concerts usually start at 10pm, and can be found at the fabulously renovated Teatre Principal (www.teatreprincipal.com) and the Auditorium (www.auditoriumpalma.com) – home to the Ciutat de Palma Symphony Orchestra. There is one original-language cinema – Cine Ciutat, on the north side of town at Carrer de l'Emperadriu,

Eugenia 6 – which regularly shows English-language films.

Dance

Classical or contemporary dance performances are few and far between, but there are a couple of decent salsa and samba bars, including Made in Brasil, which also offers dance classes. Flamenco isn't big in Mallorca as it has little to do with the island culture, but there are occasional guest performances in the city – keep your eyes and ears peeled.

Music

Music thrives in Palma, ranging from classical guitar competitions and jazz festivals to piano recitals. There is also a strong jazz and blues scene in the small bars of the old city. Free outdoor concerts – jazz, rock and classical – are held in the beautiful setting of the Parc de la Mar (walk 1, see page 30) on some summer evenings. A bar serves drinks and snacks, and there's a party atmosphere.

Summer is the time for music festivals, most held in beautiful historic buildings. The best known

Folk dancing and music

one is the Deià International Music Festival (www.dimf.com). Most performances are in the stunning setting of Son Marroig. The Chopin Festival is held in the cloister of La Cartuja in Valldemossa (www.festival chopin.com); and the Festival de Pollença (www.festivalpollenca.com) attracts international musicians to the lovely cloister of Sant Domingo. There is a summer music festival with performances in Palma's Castell de Bellver and in the Jardins Fundació March in Cala Ratjada (www.fundacionbmarch.es). Palma also stages events in various venues as part of the Jazz Voyeur Festival (www.jazzvoyeurfestival.es).

Bars and cafés

Bar-hopping is the favoured nocturnal pursuit in Palma, and few things beat kicking back on a terrace with a glass of wine, a beer or *café con hielo* on a balmy summer night. Café Lírico at Avinguda Antoni Maura 6 or La Bóveda nearby at Carrer Boteria 3 fill up around 10pm and stay full until their doors close at 2–3am. If it's cocktails you seek, don't miss Ábaco (see page 102). It's a Palma institution – kitsch, camp, exotic and expensive, and no trip is complete without experiencing it.

Nightlife

In the large resorts, notably Magaluf, clubs and discos keep going all night, catering mainly to a very young and very raucous tourist crowd. Generally speaking, the scene is less classy (and drug-fuelled) than in Ibiza, and the best way to find out what's happening is to pick up leaflets in bars in Palma and the rest of the island.

In Palma itself the scene is rather more sophisticated, attracting an older, well-heeled crowd who like their dancing after dinner, their cocktails made with premium liquor and to be in bed by 3am. There are some places where you can dance until dawn, such as super-hip beach clubs like Puro Beach (www.purobeach.com) at Cala Estancia or the Beach Club (www.balnearioilletas.com) at Illetes.

Remember that wherever you go, the action doesn't really start until around midnight.

Dinner and spectacle

A phenomenon that arrived a few decades ago is the 'dinner and spectacle' evening and despite the rather cheesy overtones they are immensely popular. They range from those suitable for children, such as at Pirates in Magaluf (https://piratesadventure.com/en), to a rather swankier affair at the Casino in the Centro Porto Pi (www.portopicentro.es). The dress code is smart-casual, and you will need your passport to get in. Book tickets in advance, especially during peak season.

Being able to dine outdoors is part of the Spanish idyll

Activities

It's easy to think of Mallorca as a place with a great beach and little else, but the island is blessed with a diverse landscape that makes it perfect for any number of outdoor pursuits and sports activities.

Of all the Balearic Islands, Mallorca's terrain is the most rewarding, ranging from the gently undulating hills across Es Pla (the central plains), which are ideal for cyclists, to ancient stone paths that crisscross the Tramuntana mountain range. You can ramble along cliff paths leading down to secluded bays or tee off on some of the world's most stunning golf courses. Highlights are included within the walks and tours' sections, but see below to get some idea about what else is out there.

Beach-hopping

There are some 80-odd beaches on Mallorca, ranging from wild and windswept to idyllic, isolated coves, and everything in between. Beaches around the Bay of Palma are fairly busy, trendy and well catered for in terms of bars, restaurants and beach clubs. West coast beaches are less accessible and shingle rather than sand, but great if you like isolation. The north coast is mainly family-oriented, with a few hidden gems at the northeastern tip. The east coast is largely built up, save for some less-developed strands like that at Canyamel and the south, once you get away from the Bay of Palma, is wild

and unspoilt and all the lovelier for it. Naturists should head to the designated nudist beaches at Es Trenc (the central part), El Mago (signposted from the road to Cap de Cala Figuera, Bay of Palma) and Cala S'Almunia (walkable from Cala Lombards heading south).

Climbing

More extreme sports (deep-water soloing for instance) are starting to take off, but climbing has already gained a firm foothold among more adventurous travellers, thanks to the stunning landscape. Much of it is done on already bolted-in limestone surfaces, a lot of which rise up spectacularly from the sea. Nearly all of it is in the northwest Tramuntana.

Cycling

Over the past few years Mallorca has become a massive destination for keen and professional cyclists – Tour de France training is done here, for example – particularly across the central plains. Good roads and varied terrain mean it offers something for everyone. Tour operators like Mallorca Cycling (www.mallorcacycling.co.uk) are a good way to go, but you could approach it

Windsurfing

at a luxurious level, for example at Port Blue Hotels (www.portbluehotels.com), which offers state-of-the-art kit as well as experienced guides and trainers.

Golf

There are 20 golf courses on Mallorca. Some of the finest, including the prestigious Son Vida, are clustered around the Bay of Palma. You can get discounted green fees through the website www.simplymallorcagolf.com, as well as information on each course. Many hotels offer golfing packages, and there's a good range of places to choose from. You can also pay day green fees at most of the courses.

Hiking

The Dry Stone Route (GR-221; Ruta de la Pedra en Sec) is the most popular hiking trail on Mallorca and takes you through the entire Tramuntana (about eight days). There are five refuges to stay in en route, and www.camins-mallorca.info has excellent information, including downloadable maps and route planners. If you want to do something less strenuous, there are innumerable well-marked trails all over the island, and new and improved paths are opening all the time.

Hot-air ballooning

The most spectacular and memorable way to see the island, riding high over the plains and mountains and deep blue sea, is not as inaccessible

Birdwatching

Mallorca is a great place for birdwatching. Migrant birds visit in spring, and some stay throughout the summer. As many as 200 different species have been recorded. The place where you are most likely to see a wide variety is the Parc Natural S'Albufera on the Bay of Alcúdia. The Parc Natural de Mondragó in the southeast is another good spot, especially for seabirds, and you may spot black vultures as well as other more common birds of prey in the wild Tramuntana region. For details, go to www.mallorcabirdwatching.com.

as you might imagine. Flights even include champagne. Check www.balloonflightsspain.com.

Watersports

The main activities are sailing, windsurfing and scuba-diving. Palma is a good place to charter a sailing boat if you want to go island hopping (www.mallorcanautic.com). The best area for scuba-diving is the west coast, where sheer cliffs and sheltered bays attract the most diverse sea life. West Coast Divers, www.divinginmajorca.com, offer a wide selection of dives. The near-constant winds of the Cap de Ses Salines attract serious windsurfers, but learners are better off on the north coast; check www.windfriends.com.

Hiking in the hills

Snorkelling in crystal clear water

Chronology

Mallorca has been ruled by Romans and Moors, gained and lost independence, stood up to Napoleon and supported Franco's Falangists. Today, it's one of the most affluent islands in the Mediterranean.

The remains of a Talayotic village in Menorca

Early period

2700 BC Neolithic pastoralists roam Mallorca, colonizing Menorca about four centuries later.
1500 BC The islanders learn how to work bronze; the Talayotic period begins.
800 BC Greeks displace the Phoenicians as the dominant power in the western Mediterranean.
700 BC Carthaginians begin to colonize the Balearics.

146 BC Final defeat of the Carthaginians by Rome.
123 BC–400 AD The Romans invade and Mallorca is absorbed into the Roman Empire. It is named 'Balearis Major' and towns including Palmaria (Palma) and Pollentia (Alcúdia) are established.
902–905 AD The Moors conquer the Balearics. They introduce many new crops, including the orange, lemon, peach, apricot and fig.
11th century AD Moorish Spain disintegrates into squabbling *taifas*, or petty fiefdoms.

The 13th to 18th centuries

1229 Jaume I of Aragón and Catalunya captures Mallorca from the Moors; a bloodbath ensues.
1276 Death of Jaume I and creation of the independent Kingdom of Mallorca ruled by Jaume II.
1324–44 Reign of Jaume III, bringing economic prosperity.
1344 Troops of Pedro IV of Aragón invade and reincorporate the islands into the Kingdom of Aragón.
1479 Kingdoms of Castile and Aragón, including Mallorca, united. Economic decline begins in the Balearics.

Roman ruins of Pollentia at Alcúdia

1492 The fall of Granada, the last Moorish kingdom in Spain; Columbus reaches the Americas.
1494 The Treaty of Tordesillas divides the New World between Spain and Portugal.
16th century Spain emerges as a single political entity, with the Inquisition acting as a unifying, albeit oppressive force; as Spain turns towards the Americas, the Balearics fall into economic decline.
1700 Felipe de Bourbón ascends to the throne. Beginning of the War of Spanish Succession.

The 19th century

1808–13 Spain's War of Independence against Napoleonic troops.
1837 First steamship line between Mallorca and the mainland.
1879–98 Spain in further decline; the arrival of the phylloxera grape pest ravages Mallorca's vineyards.

The 20th century to the present

1936–9 Spanish Civil War. Mallorca is seized by Franco's Nationalists.
1939–75 The dictatorship of General Franco – political oppression and the suppression of the Catalan language.
1960s Mallorca's airport is built and subsequent mass tourism brings an influx of capital, but great environmental damage.
1975 Juan Carlos I becomes king after the death of Franco.

1983 The Balearics become an autonomous province. Mallorquín is made the official language.
1985 Abortion legalized; Catholic priests are horrified.
1986 Spain joins the European Community (now the EU).
2000s The government initiates measures to encourage eco-friendly tourism and move the island's image upmarket.
2002 The euro becomes the official currency of Spain.
2005 Same-sex marriage made legal in Spain; Catholic priests horrified – again.
2015 Left-wing Partido Socialista Obrero Español (PSOE) and coalition Més per Mallorca (Més) form the new regional government in the Balearics headed by Francina Armengol (PSOE). A record 11.6 million international tourists visit the Balearic Islands.
2016 Sustainable Tourism Tax (better known as 'eco tax') is introduced on the Balearic Islands to raise funds for environmental and heritage protection, as well as for investment in sustainable tourism.
2020–22 COVID-19 hits Spain hard in the spring of 2020; national lockdowns followed by a successful vaccination programme reduces the risk of the virus.
July 2024 Palma: thousands of islanders march against mass tourism, highlighting the difficulties they face from the lack of affordable housing through to environmental degradation.

Depiction of the thirteenth-century Conquest of Mallorca

TRIP PLANS

WALK 1
Historic Palma

This half-day walk offers a distilled version of the history of Palma. Explore the narrow lanes of the medieval Jewish quarter – now also home to chic boutiques and trendy restaurants – and add drama with a peek at the impressive cathedral, serene Arabic Baths and a king's secret garden.

DISTANCE: Approximately 3km
TIME: Leisurely half-day
START: Parc del Mar
END: S'Hort del Rei (The King's Garden)
POINTS TO NOTE: This walk is ideal for first-time visitors to Palma, showcasing the oldest, prettiest part of the old city, which is known as Sa Calatrava. Because the sights along it are open year round, it works at any time of year and could easily connect with all or some of walk 2, if you wanted to cram a lot into a day.

Set around a sheltered bay, **Palma** is a large, cosmopolitan city, with around 420,500 inhabitants – almost half the permanent population of Mallorca. It is very much a Mediterranean city, with palm trees and bushes of fragrant oleander, outdoor cafés with colourful awnings, and yachts bobbing in the bay. It's smart and urbane, with designer boutiques, smart restaurants and chic art galleries hidden in narrow alleys.

The city also has a colourful cultural history. Founded by the Romans in 123 BC as Palmeria, it was a major trading centre even before the arrival of the Moors in 902 AD. Seeing the city's potential, they built mosques (one where the cathedral now stands), bathhouses and other tokens of civilised life.

This walk starts where the twenty-first century and the Middle Ages meet, at the Parc del Mar.

Parc del Mar

Start your walk at the entrance to the Moorish Walls at the western end of the **Parc del Mar** ❶, which gives the most commanding view. The contemporary concrete and wood landscaping provides a striking contrast to the old city and the sea beyond. In the middle is an artificial lake designed to reflect Palma's imposing cathedral, an essential stop for photography enthusiasts. It is

"La Seu" cathedral in Palma

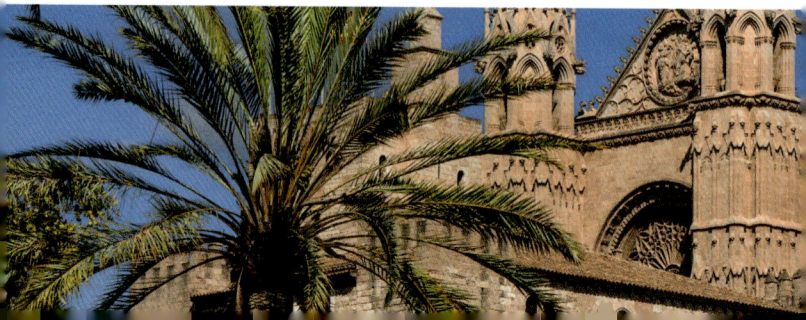

also home to a number of modern sculptures, including a vibrant mural by Joan Miró. Head west along the Passeig Marítim for breakfast or a coffee at **Cappuccino Grand Café**, see ①, before you start.

Follow the walls around to the east and you will eventually reach a plain arch – the **Porta de la Portella** ❷ – the official gateway to the Casc Antic (Old City) under Arabic rule and the heart of the Call (Jewish quarter) during the thirteenth and fourteenth centuries. Straight ahead at Carrer de la Portella 5 is the **Museu de Mallorca** ❸ (tel: 971 597 995). Housed in the resplendent mansion Ca La Gran Cristiana, it is well worth a stop to take a peek at Roman remains, Gothic and Islamic art, and get a sense of the rich history of this comparatively small city.

Palma's Jewish heart

This compact, car-free neighbourhood of narrow cobblestoned streets was home to one of the most prolific Jewish communities in the entire Mediterranean in the Middle Ages, although Jews had been here since Roman times. This cultural mix accounts in some part for the diverse architectural styles that make up one of the most handsome cities in the Mediterranean, much of which spun out from a sacred hill in the centre known as **Monte Sión** ❹ – now the site of a church.

One of the great Jewish celebrities of the fourteenth century was the cartographer Jafuda Cresques (Jaume Ribes), who was credited with drawing up the first Catalan Atlas as well as the maps used by Christopher Columbus, who himself may well have been of Jewish descent. His house still stands on Carrer Botones, due east of the Church of Monte Sión. It is not open to the public, but there is a small monument of Jafuda.

Arabic baths

From the museum, turn right onto Carrer Pureza and immediately right again onto Carrer Serra and you'll find one of the last remaining vestiges of the Moorish occupation. The **Banys Arabs** ❺ (Arabic Baths; Carrer Serra 7), which once housed the hot baths, are well preserved, with a brick cupola pinpricked with tiny skylights. The secret, shaded gardens also provide a superb retreat if you're looking for somewhere to escape with a book for an hour or two.

Catholic churches

Head north along Carrer de Santa Clara, then right onto Carrer Pont y Vich and Carrer Pau Nadal and you'll pop out on pretty Plaça Sant Francesc, where there is a chapel of the same name. The **Basílica de Sant Francesc** ❻ is something of a hidden treasure, notable for having beautiful cloisters, with delicately carved columns and arches. It is also the final resting place of Ramon Llull (1235–1315), who was credited with penning the first great literary work in Catalan.

Palmas's oldest café

A couple of streets away heading north, the beautifully tiled eighteenth-century **Can Joan de S'Aigo**, see ❷, on Carrer de Can Sanç 10, was the artist Joan Miró's favourite café, and there is no better place for a quick pick-me-up.

Palma's Parliament

Wiggle your way westwards over onto Carrer Colóm, then head south to the **Ajuntament** ❼ (City Hall; www.palma.cat; fortnightly tours in English, booking essential, tel: 618 914 517) with a striking overhanging roof, supported by carved beams. Enter the street-level hallway and you will get to see a couple of ceremonial Mallorcan *gigantes* (giants) built of papier-mâché and hauled out for every local celebration. Further down the street, the magnificent ochre colonnades of the **Parlament de les Illes Baleares** ❽ have been the hub of city politics since the seventeenth century.

A hard left along the Carrer de l'Almudaina brings you to another of the city's original Arabic gates, the **Arc de l'Almudaina** ❾, which some experts suggest could date back to Roman times. If you're hungry, the excellent **Las Olas** bistro, see ❸, is just

Ajuntament (City Hall)

up the road on Carrer Fortuny and is a great choice for a casual lunch.

Cathedral by the sea

Head back down Carrer Palau Reial and the city's crowning glory, the cathedral, known simply as **La Seu** ❿ (Plaça de la Seu s/n; www.catedraldemallorca.org; charge) towers up before you (Seu means a bishop's seat). Like many places of religious significance in much of Spain, its first stone was laid on the site of a former mosque, in this case by Jaume I in 1229, and it took hundreds of years to complete. It encompasses a range of architectural styles, from the Gothic features of the sixteenth century right through to Modernista flourishes added by legendary Barcelona architect Antoni Gaudí between 1902 and 1914. Check out his wrought-iron 'crown of thorns' – the baldachin – over the altar.

The immense sense of space and light here is largely due to seven rose windows, the most spectacular of which has a 12m (40ft) diameter. Externally, its flying buttresses give it a fortress-like appearance, while its watery surroundings make it seem like it's floating out to sea. Take the time to walk around it, for it is truly extraordinary from any angle and at any time of day. The cathedral **museum** (same hours as cathedral) is worth a look too – it contains, among other curios, Jaume I's dainty portable altar.

Royal palaces

Next door to the cathedral is the **Palau de l'Almudaina** ⓫ (www.patrimonio nacional.es; charge), built on the site of a Moorish fortress. It was revamped by Jaume I in Gothic style and since 1985 has been the official residence of the king of Spain when he is in Mallorca. The fourteenth-century Capella de Santa Ana and thirteenth-century Sala del Tinell (Throne Room) are the principal highlights, along with some impressive Flemish tapestries. It also has a very pretty courtyard (Patio del Rei).

Palma's coat of arms, as seen at the Palau, features a spread-eagled bat above the shield. Various legends surround its significance, but the most popular is that a bat flew into a drum one night while Christian soldiers lay slumbering. The noise it made woke them up just in time to save themselves from a marauding Moorish army, which contributed to their eventual reconquest of the island.

Shipyards and stock exchange

Head down the steps between the cathedral and the Almudaina, to what was once the royal shipyards. The site is now occupied by the **Museu Ses Voltes** ⓬ (times vary according to exhibitions; free), set into the city walls and devoted to works by contemporary Mallorcan artists.

From here head back along the walls and cross over Avinguda Antoni

S'Hort del Rei (King's Garden)

St George statue on the Basílica de Sant Francesc

Food and Drink

❶ Cappuccino Grand Café
Passeig Maritím 1;
www.cappuccino.com; €
This chic café is one of a small
chain with several branches in
attractive locations throughout the
city. It's a great place for breakfast
and a *café con leche* on the sunny
terrace before you start your walk,
and also does good lunches.

❷ Can Joan de S'Aigo
Carrer de Can Sanç 10;
www.canjoandesaigo.
webs-sites.com; €
Think traditional charm at this
300-year-old café. Settle into one
of the velvet banquettes for hot
chocolate and an *ensaimada* (the
snail-shaped pastry sprinkled
with icing sugar) on chilly days.
If it's hot, you can get a scoop of
almond ice cream to take away.

❸ Las Olas
Carrer Fortuny 5; tel: 971 21 49 05; €€
A great local bistro that offers
an excellent value, three-course
menú del día. Expect creative
Mediterranean dishes such as
watermelon gazpacho and roast
bacalao (salt cod) with apple *alioli*.
Just the ticket after a morning
stomping around the sights.

Maura to the Plaça de Sa Llotja,
and you'll come to the whimsical-
looking turreted **Sa Llotja** ⓭ (open
when exhibitions are on; free), built
by Guillem Sagrera in the fifteenth
century as the merchants' stock
exchange. Today, this elegant Gothic
building is used for art exhibitions,
a role for which its beautiful airy
interior is well suited. Next door,
the seventeenth-century **Consulat
del Mar** ⓮ was built as a maritime
court – today used as provincial
government offices – and is easily
identified by the cannon and a
large anchor standing outside it.

A king's garden
Retrace your steps along Carrer
Marina and Carrer Boteria (parallel
to the Passeig Marítim), turning
north onto Avinguda Antoni Maura
to the **S'Hort del Rei** ⓯ (King's
Garden), a park filled with pools,
fountains and shady greenery,
among which stand several arresting
modern sculptures, and a bronze
hondero (the name of the early
sling-throwers – in ancient times,
Balearic islanders were famed for
their skills with a sling in battle).

At the upper end, near Miró's
famous sculpture called *Personatge*
– popularly known as simply
'The Egg' – is a pleasant little bar
with tables and chairs outside,
the perfect spot for a nice cold
beer at the end of your walk.

Tapestry in Palau de l'Almudaina

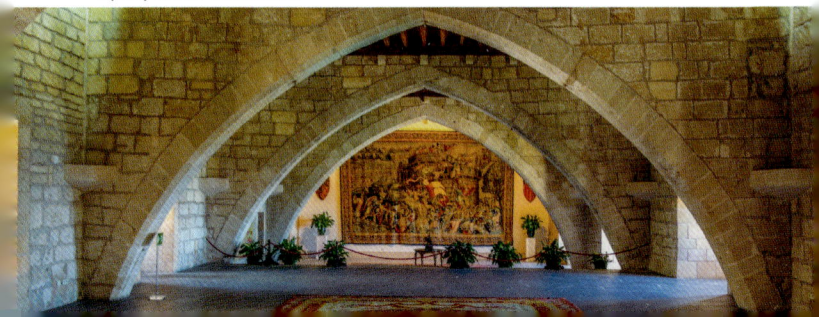

WALK 2
Palma's galleries

Despite its modest size, Palma has gained a reputation as one of the more important art destinations in Spain. It has several privately owned collections as well as a few world-class galleries.

DISTANCE: 1.5km
TIME: One day or a leisurely half-day
START: Es Baluard
END: Plaça d'Espanya
POINTS TO NOTE: This walk is great for out-of-season visits when the museums and galleries are quieter. The first two galleries are within easy walking distance of each other, while the Pilar and Joan Miró Foundation is best accessed by bus. You could also connect to walk 7 by hopping on the Sóller train at Plaça d'Espanya.

Over the last hundred years Mallorca has become increasingly prosperous, a fact highlighted by its love of art. There are large galleries, outdoor sculpture parks and private collections stashed away in stately homes and mansions. This walk covers Palma's big three.

Es Baluard

The jewel in Palma's artistic crown is located in a former military stronghold, built in the early sixteenth century to protect the town against marauders. In 1952 it passed into private hands, and after a lengthy period of stagnation it was slated for destruction. A horrified public stepped in and eventually it was given to Palma City Council, who decided to turn it into a modern art museum, **Es Baluard Museu d'Art Modern** ❶ (Plaça Porta de Santa Catalina 10; www.esbaluard.org; charge), which opened in 2004.

A local architect's firm, On Diseño, was commissioned to integrate the ancient walls within a more modern design, and the result is a stunning contemporary gallery showcasing rotating exhibitions, that attracts big names from all over the world. It's worth setting aside a couple of hours just to appreciate the space fully.

The original stone walls of the fortress soften the effects of the steel and concrete, giving it an unexpectedly organic feel. Spacious and light-filled, it seamlessly combines interior and exterior spaces, encouraging visitors to interact with the building as well as the art within it. A walkway that wraps around the roof affords spellbinding views of the sea and city.

Es Baluard Museu d'Art Modern

The 'Aljub'

The main exhibition space for concerts and installations occupies the former 'Aljub', a Moorish name for a freshwater reservoir. Until the mid-twentieth century, it supplied fresh water to the entire Sant Pere district, channelled from the La Vila spring in the town of Esporles along what is now Bonaire Street. Should you start to fade, the rooftop café and terrace offer sweeping views of the port.

Museu Fundación Juan March

From Es Baluard it takes just 15 minutes to walk northeast across the old city to the splendid **Museu Fundació Juan March ❷** (Sant Miquel 11; www.march.es; free).

Weave up Carrer Olivera, through Plaça Santa Cruz and along Carrer Paz to Plaça Rei Joan Carlcs, then turn right along La Unió to the arcaded Plaça Major and north onto Carrer Sant Miquel, a pretty and highly enjoyable walk, which will lead you to the seventeenth-century mansion Can Gallard des Canyar, now home to an impressive selection of the March family's extensive private art collection.

The March legacy

Juan March made his fortune in banking in the late 1930s, when he became known as 'Franco's Banker' after funding his right-wing nationalist party. His extreme Conservatism clearly paid off, because by 1955 he was reckoned

Exhibits in the Fundació Juan March

Miró Foundation

Bus numbers 47 or 46 take you straight from the Plaça d'Espanya to the Fundació Pilar i Joan Miró a Mallorca (Carrer Saridakis 29; www.miromallorca.com/en; charge) in about 30 minutes. It is a gleaming white building designed by Rafel Moneo.

The prolific collection totals 118 paintings, 275 mixed media pieces, 1,512 drawings and 35 sculptures, covering the period of 1908–81. It also includes his personal collection of works by other artists and sculptors, newspaper and magazine clippings and other tokens of inspiration.

Food and Drink

● L'Antiquari

Carrer Arabí 5; tel: 871 572 313; €
Hip retro café noted for its quiches, ham and cheese platters and toasted sandwiches. It's also a great place for a drink in the evening and there are regular live music concerts.

● Marc Fosh Restaurant

Carrer de la Missió, 7A;
www.marcfosh.com; €€€–€€€€
Acclaimed chef Marc Fosh's Michelin-starred restaurant offers a three-course lunch menu using fresh ingredients and an inspired à la carte menu with dishes like venison with pumpkin and sea bream with olive oil parmentier, raisins, spinach and pine nuts.

to be one of the richest men in the world, and his legacy lives on not only in the form of the bank which still carries the family name, but in various cultural guises around the island.

Home of the Spanish vanguard

What is most striking about the collection is the sheer range. Dark expressionism by Miquel Barceló stands shoulder to shoulder with metal sculptures by Eduardo Chillida; surrealist and technical paintings by Salvador Dalí alongside big bolts of primary colour by Antoni Tàpies. These are just a few of the big names. There is also a permanent space dedicated solely to Picasso's etchings. Allow an hour or so to absorb it fully, then treat yourself to a snack at **L'Antiquari**, see ●, or a more substantial lunch at **Marc Fosh Restaurant**, see ●.

Plaça d'Espanya

To continue to the **Fundació Pilar i Joan Miró a Mallorca** ●, head for the Plaça d'Espanya straight up Carrer de Sant Miquel. Turn right at Plaça Porta Pintada, which pops you out on Plaça d'Espanya.

A lecture in Es Baluard

Canvasses at the Fundació Pilar i Joan Miró

WALK 3
Palma for foodies

Mallorca has established itself as one of the hottest food destinations in Europe, with Palma at the head of the table. This walk wiggles through the centre from the Santa Catalina market to a well-stocked cheese shop.

DISTANCE: 2.5km
TIME: Half-day
START: Mercat de Santa Catalina
END: Sa Formatgeria
POINTS TO NOTE: Do this walk in the morning when market produce is at its freshest and you can work up a healthy appetite for lunch (on Sunday the featured places are shut). You could split it in two and do your shopping in the morning, before linking up with walks 1 or 2.

There is something thrilling about shopping for food in a foreign place, and Palma is no exception.

Mercat de Santa Catalina

The **Mercat de Santa Catalina**
❶ (Plaça Navegació; www. mercatdesantacatalina.com; closed Sun) occupies an entire block of the Santa Catalina neighbourhood. Rub shoulders with local people, learn about the fish and seafood and see what fruit and vegetables are in season. Shop for cheese and sausages and olive oils at the richly laden Charcuterie Selecta Izquierdo stall (www.charcuteriaizquierdo.com); for *pimentón* and saffron, marcona almonds and pine nuts, go to Especias Crespi (www.especiascrespi.com). To get really into the spirit of things, have a tapa and a mid-morning glass of wine at the bar near Carrer de Soler exit. For something more substantial, the bars and restaurants that surround the market serve solid, unpretentious food, see ❶.

Specialist shops

Cross back into the centre of the old town for the best of the rest. The most direct route is along the La Llotja section of the old walls (see walk 1), left onto Avenida Antoni Maura and Carrer Conquistador, and left again onto Carrer Santo Domingo. Right at its head you'll find the **Colmado Santo Domingo** ❷ (www.colmadosantodomingo. com), one of the city's oldest shops and purveyors of the finest *porc negre* artisan sausage in town.

Minutes away, **La Pajarita** ❸ (Carrer Sant Nicolau 2–4, www.la pajaritabomboneria.com) is an old-

Traditional oil biscuits and cheese

fashioned sweet and cake shop and the place to pick up a giant *ensaimada* packed into a cardboard box and tied up with string. The shop interior is a delight, with crystal chandeliers, Modernista tiles and a counter piled high with jewel-coloured sweet treats.

Continue along Carrer Sant Nicolau, turning right onto Carrer Mercado where the **Chocolat Factory** ❹ (Plaça d'es Mercat 9; www.chocolatfactory. com) has an extraordinary range of products, ranging from truffles and bonbons to gourmet, single-estate chocolate and children's snacks.

From here it's a leisurely stroll northeast to Carrer del Oms and **Sa Formatgeria** at No. 30 ❺ (www.sa formatgeria.com), which sells a

wide variety of cheeses including several from Mallorca such as Ruat organic goat's cheese. They also stock wine, olive oil and other regional products from the Balearic Islands.

Food and Drink

❶ El Perrito
Carrer Anníbal 20; tel: 613 006 573; €€
Popular for post-shopping coffee, brunch and laid-back lunches at the weekend, this place positively bristles with atmosphere. Try to nab a seat out on the pavement terrace where you can watch the world go by.

Find classic Mallorcan sweet treats at La Pajarita

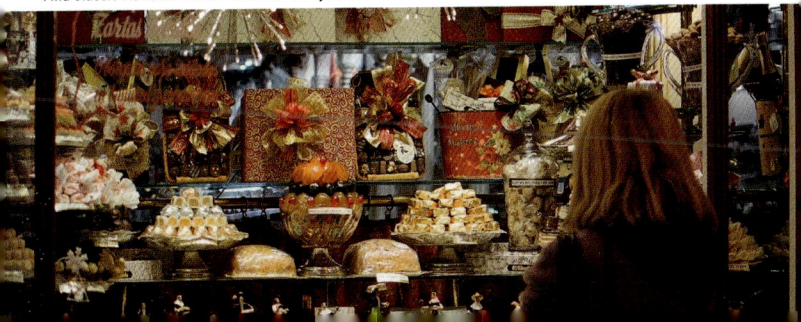

TOUR 4
Andratx to Banyalbufar

The southwest is a curious mix, where mass tourism meets the glitzy jet set then leads on to sleepy villages, terraced hillsides and glorious clifftop views. The tour can be crammed into a day, but it is best to stay overnight.

DISTANCE: 33km
TIME: 1–2 days
START: Port Adriano
END: Banyalbufar
POINTS TO NOTE: This tour should be travelled by car, but includes a possible boat trip and two hikes. It's best done in the summer if you want to make the boat trip to Sa Dragonera and swim in the sea, while spring and autumn are preferable for hiking. If you do plan to include either of the hikes featured, note they are fairly strenuous and not suitable for small children.

This tour takes you from the swish port of Port Adriano to sleepy Sant Elm, then via a coast road with jaw-dropping views to a ruined monastery and the terraced hillsides of Banyalbufar, where there are some excellent restaurants.

Port Adriano

To get to **Port Adriano ❶** (Santa Ponça s/n; www.portadriano.com),

drive west along the main highway, the Ma-1, from Palma for around 10km. Turn left for Santa Ponça and it is well signposted from there. Built in 1992, Port Adriano was handed over to French designer Philippe Starck in 2007 to be remodelled as the Balearic power port for super yachts, complete with a heliport and luxury shops and restaurants. Visitors can enjoy its unique Starck design while strolling the docks, admiring the pleasure palaces of the rich and famous. There are plenty of places to grab a cup of coffee before continuing.

Adriano to Andratx

The Ma-1 continues northwards to **Andratx ❷**, which is spread messily out beneath the twin peaks of the S'Esclop mountain (926m). The town sits at the heart of a fertile agricultural region and is refreshingly low-key in terms of tourism. Originally founded as a refuge for Christian settlers, it was the home of both the bishop of Barcelona and King Jaume I in the thirteenth

Port Adriano

great deal to see or do here except on Wednesdays, which is market day, but it's a pleasant enough town for a stroll.

S'Arracó's colonial architecture

On the western edge of Andratx is the tiny village of **S'Arracó** ❸. Once said to have taken nine hours by cart to reach from Palma, it is difficult to imagine now, but the village retains its atmosphere and is a good place to get a glimpse of the *casas de indianos* (houses built by Mallorcans returning from the colonies), now highly coveted second homes.

Paradise islands

Continuing west from S'Arracó you will come to the pretty port town of **Sant Elm** ❹ – the gateway to the rugged island of **Sa Dragonera** ❺ which apparently gets its name from its appearance, as it resembles the back of a dragon emerging out of the sea. Once the hideout of Redbeard the pirate, these days it's the favoured haunt of a multitude of

century, and at the top of the town, above the Plaça del Pou, the towering walls of the fortress-like church of Santa Maria still stand proud and strong. Check out the brilliant Centro Cultural Andratx (Estanyera, 2; www.ccandratx.com; charge), the largest centre of contemporary art on the island, set in stunning surroundings. There are also artists' workshops, a café and bookshop on site. Other than that, there's not a

Andratx

Sant Elm

Cliff walk

For keen walkers the most rewarding way to get to Banyalbufar from Estellencs is to walk along the cliff paths of the GR-221 (www.gr221.info). Editorial Alpina provides detailed maps of the region, priced at around €15. It takes a good day to get there and back, but it's an unforgettable walk with a couple of opportunities to jump into the sea at the start and finish of the trail. A picnic, plenty of water and sunscreen are essential.

Lilford's lizards which enjoy lounging around in the sun. *Margarita* boat tours (www.crucerosmargarita.com), run back and forth to the island every 30 minutes between April and September, and between February and March and in October. It is a proper paradise for those who make the trip – mainly walkers and birdwatchers who come to see the rare Eleanora's falcon and impressive numbers of seabirds. Scattered around are a number of little islets, perfect for snorkelling and bathing. Remember to take a picnic – if you're going on a Wednesday, stop off at Andratx's weekly market to pick up some goodies – or you can always head back to **Arasa**, see ❶, for lunch in Sant Elm as you won't find anywhere to eat on the island.

The Sa Trapa trail

Back in Sant Elm you can walk to the ruins of the ancient **Sa Trapa** ❻ monastery without leaving dry land. It is a popular walk and well signposted, but it's not suitable for small children and requires a certain fitness level – expect to take at least four hours to do the round trip. The scenery, particularly when the spring flowers are in full bloom, is spectacular, and the views of Sa Dragonera are second to none.

Andratx to Estellencs

Back in Andratx, continue driving north in the direction of Banyalbufar on Ma-1. At around 99km you will spot the famed **Mirador de Ricard Roca** ❼, which has jaw-dropping views of the deep-blue Mediterranean, providing you can see past the tour buses. It may be better to bypass the crowds and keep going until you reach **Estellencs** ❽ (pronounced 'Es-ta-yencs'). The village is postcard-perfect, with narrow, cobblestoned streets and pretty honey-coloured stone cottages, their window boxes spilling over with geraniums and ferns.

Cala Estellencs

If you are spreading this tour over two days and have booked accommodation in Estellencs, end your day with a dip at pint-sized **Cala Estellencs** ❾. Take a hard

Watchtower at the Mirador de Ses Ànimes

Food and Drink

1 Arasa
Avinguda Jaime I 6, Sant Elm;
tel: 971 239 272; €€
This simple seaside restaurant serves
some of the freshest fish and seafood
in the area and is great for tapas
and salads. The terrace gives views
straight over to Sa Dragonera, and
it's a great place to kick back and
do nothing for a couple of hours.

2 Ca'n Toni Moreno
Carrer des Port d'es Canonge 2,
Banyalbufar; tel: 971 610 426; €€€
A short detour from Banyalbufar

is this pretty shingle beach with
one lone, inauspicious-looking
restaurant. The fish is first rate,
particularly the *caldereta de langosta*
(a local lobster stew enriched
with tomatoes and saffron).

3 Hotel Mar i Vent
Carrer Major 49, Banyalbufar
www.hotelmarivent.com; €€
It's worth calling ahead to bag a
spot on the spectacular terrace,
which occupies a beautiful position
on the edge of the cliff. The food
here is simple Mallorquín fare
for the most part, with Sunday
lunch paella the star turn.

left downhill onto Carrer Eusebi Pascual on entering the village, and follow it down to the sea (about 2km). The rocky inlet and beach are ringed by tiny boathouses where local fishermen keep their nets and gear, and it's a wonderfully secluded spot for a sunset swim.

Estellencs to Banyalbufar

This section of the drive passes another viewpoint, the **Mirador de Ses Ànimes**, where there are stunning views of the coast from a sixteenth-century watchtower, the Torre Verger, which was built during the time when Mallorca was regularly being attacked by pirates; throughout the

tour you get plenty of opportunity to admire the ancient Moorish terracing of the steep hillsides of pretty **Banyalbufar** ❿. On the surrounding embankment villagers once cultivated the now-legendary *malvasia* wine. Although the wine is no more, its name lives on in local parlance as a synonym for 'marvellous'.

If you arrive here in time for lunch, and we recommend that you should, **Ca'n Toni Moreno**, see ❷, does great fish right on the beach. And if you arrive closer to sunset, **Hotel Mar-i-Vent**, see ❸, which was a chic, summer retreat for well-heeled Palma residents during the 1940s, is now a good bet for drinks or dinner.

Banyalbufar

TOUR 5
Villages of the Tramuntana

This beautiful, but relatively unknown region takes in some of the most spectacular vistas and prettiest villages of the Serra de Tramuntana.

DISTANCE: 37km
TIME: 1 day
START: Bunyola
END: Lloseta
POINTS TO NOTE: The villages are linked by the Ma-2110, which makes the tour easy to follow, but the road is full of hairpin bends, so it's slow going. If you don't have time for the whole tour, or don't want to rent a car, take the Sóller train from Palma to Bunyola (www.trendesoller.com), which links to walk 7.

The pretty villages of Bunyola, Orient, Alaró and Lloseta can all be used as jumping-off points for a variety of well-marked hiking trails. If you want to spend a couple of days exploring the area, Orient, with good restaurants and hotels, is the best base.

Bunyola

Driving into **Bunyola** ❶ on the Ma-11 from Palma, the first thing you notice is the striking yellow-tiled spire and bright green shutters of the Modernista Villa Francisca, which gives a sense of the bourgeois nature of these mountain villages. In the nineteenth century it was known for its wine (the name is from the Arabic word for vineyard) and was quickly adopted by the upper classes as an escape from the city during the Belle Epoque.

Today, the village is popular with second-home owners, but has largely escaped the ravages of more conspicuous forms of mass tourism. Bunyola is a sweet place for a cup of coffee, especially on Saturday mornings when the market takes over the main plaza. For walkers, the wooded glades that surround the town make for some good rambling. Paths are signposted from the train station, but if it's serious hiking you're after, continue on to Orient.

Orient

Leave Bunyola on the Ma-2100 with the majestic Serra d'Alfàbia rising up to your left. Once over the pass, the descent into the lush green fields of the Vall d'Orient is breathtaking, and the small village of **Orient** ❷, is no less lovely.

The highlight is the mysterious trail to the **Salt del Freu** ❸ – a 25m-high

Bunyola's distinctive green shutters

waterfall and misty river that runs through a forest of ancient oaks.

Alaró

Continuing towards **Alaró ❹**, the road runs between two tabletop mountains: S'Alcadena to the left and the Puig d'Alaró to the right, with the ruins of the **Castell d'Alaró ❺** (www.visit.ajalaro.net/en) perched on top, offering dormitory accommodation and a restaurant with *pa amb oli* (bread and oil) and homemade cakes. One of three such structures on the island, the castle is famous for resisting for four years the Aragonese invasion of 1285, and for the grisly fate of the two commanders in charge after they capitulated.

The walk from the town of Alaró (3 hours each way) to the castle is one of the most popular on the island and well signposted. You can't drive all the way to it, but if you're looking for an easier hike, turn off at Km 18 and park at the **Es Verger** restaurant. It takes about an hour each way from there.

Lloseta

Lloseta ❻ is a pleasant spot to end your trip, with just enough interest to warrant a stroll and a look around the shops. Don't miss lunch at **Celler Can Carrossa**, see ❶, one of the most exciting little restaurants on the island.

Food and Drink

❶ Celler Can Carrossa

Carrer Nou 28, Lloseta; www.cancarrossa.com; €€€
With strong local roots, this appealing restaurant offers a tasty range of Mediterranean/Mallorcan dishes. The lamb comes especially well recommended.

Castell d'Alaró

TOUR 6
Valldemossa to Lluc

The central Tramuntana has long attracted artists, writers and musicians. This tour delves into their lives: from Frédéric Chopin and George Sand's cell in the monastery at Valldemossa and Robert Graves's writer's hideaway on the cliffs of Deià, to Mallorca's most illustrious scholar, Ramon Llull.

DISTANCE: 54km
TIME: 1 day
START: Valldemossa
END: Lluc
POINTS TO NOTE: This stretch of coast is far from undiscovered these days – come high season the tour buses and rental cars can be bumper to bumper. To avoid the crush, come in early spring or late autumn, or midweek rather than at the weekend. There are numerous places to eat en route, as well as a handful of places to stay, ranging from the luxurious to inexpensive pensions and basic rooms at the Lluc monastery.

Individual experiences can be so different. Sand's winter in the monastery in Valldemossa in 1838 was so miserable she was compelled to vent her unhappiness in a book entitled *A Winter in Mallorca*. Robert Graves had far happier experiences, pitching up in neighbouring Deià in 1929, where he stayed, off and on, for the rest of his life. Indeed, it is largely thanks to Graves that the little village of Deià became such a magnet for writers, artists and trustafarians.

Valledemossa

The truth is, **Valldemossa ❶** isn't as charming as it once was. Though still pretty enough, hordes of day-trippers from Palma have turned it into something of a theme park, albeit a fairly classy one. The main draw is the Carthusian monastery, **La Reial Cartoixa Ⓐ** (www.cartujade valldemossa.com; charge), where Frédéric Chopin and George Sand occupied two of the cells after the monks had been expelled by government decree in 1835. At least that is what was believed until a story broke in 2010 speculating that the cells purporting to be theirs were not, and the piano played during today's Chopin-themed concerts wasn't his either. What is certain is that Chopin and Sand stayed

Valldemossa

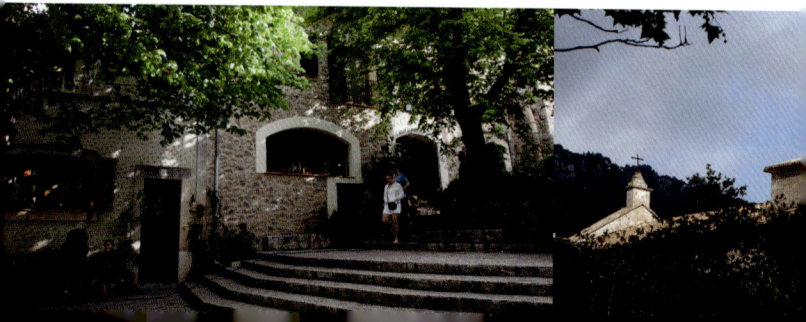

and worked somewhere within the confines of the monastery, and the Chopin concerts are worth attending regardless of whose piano it is.

Apart from said cells, there is an atmospheric pharmacy stocked with beautiful eighteenth-century ceramic jars and great views down the valley from the monks' gardens. The adjoining municipal museum has a small but excellent modern art collection, including works by Francis Bacon and Max Ernst, and the adjacent **Palau de Rei Sancho B** holds a variety of antiques and curios.

It won't take you long to get around all these, so stroll through the narrow, smooth-stoned streets around flower-decked **Plaça de Santa Catalina Tomàs C**. The square is named after Mallorca's very own saint, who was born here in 1531; there are two shrines to her in the town, and nearly every house has a tiled picture of her on the wall. Stop for a coffee and the local speciality, *coca de patata* (sugar-dusted potato buns) in **Plaça Ramón Llull D** before heading on your way.

Valldemossa to Deià

Leave town on the Avinguda Arxiduc Lluís Salvador in the direction of Sóller. When you get to the end of an avenue of plane trees the road curves sharply left for Deià, and with the first right you can head to the dinky Port de Valldemossa, a steep drive

La Reial Cartoixa

Deià

full of switchbacks and hairpin bends. The coastal Ma-10 here is similarly breathtaking, offering endless sea views to the left, and groves of ancient, gnarled olive trees among huge boulders to the right.

Son Marroig

En route to Deià you will pass **Son Marroig** ❷ (www.sonmarroig. com; charge), one of the island's great stately homes (*possessió*). It was once owned by Archduke Ludwig Salvator of Habsburg-Lorraine and Bourbon, who installed in the garden a small marble temple from which to gaze on the rock of Na Foradada, carved by nature with a keyhole-shaped aperture.

The **Sa Foradada**, see ❶, nearby is a good lunch stop, with great views and tasty homemade food.

The Graves legacy

Deià ❸ is set against the steep, rocky slopes of Puig Es Teix and is relatively lively for its size. There is little of note in the pretty, golden-stone village save for the Església de Sant Joan Bautista and its cemetery, the final resting place of Mallorca's most famous adopted son. The small flat stone says simply: 'Robert Graves, Poeta, 1895–1985'.

Graves acted as a magnet for would-be painters and writers (as well as established writers such as Anaïs Nin and the young Gabriel García Márquez, and Hollywood stars like Ava Gardner). Long after he died, the glitterati kept coming. Michael Douglas and Catherine Zeta Jones, Andrew Lloyd Webber and Pierce Brosnan all have houses nearby. Graves penned many of his major works here, including *I, Claudius*.

La Casa de Robert Graves ❹ (Carretera Deià–Sóller s/n; www.lacasaderobertgraves.org; charge) is as it was when he died, and it's worth seeing the short film made by the BBC about his life then strolling through the gardens, soaking up the tranquillity and landscape that inspired him.

Sunset from Son Marroig

For something special, it is worth the vertiginous drive down to the Cala Deià to eat at one of the best little fish shacks in Spain, **Ca's Patro March**, see ❷.

Monestir de Nostra Senyora de Lluc

Lluc is the religious centre of Mallorca and home of the island's patron saint. The monastery of **Nostra Senyora de Lluc** ❺ (www.lluc.net) is a massive site, and a destination for tens of thousands of pilgrims. But it is of interest to visitors of every creed, for its history, for the architectural interventions of Antoni Gaudí who renovated the basilica, and for its boys' choir – the Escalonia de Lluc. Clad in blue cassocks, they are considered one of the best choirs in Spain and perform renditions of the 'salvo' – a chant intended to protect the island from harm.

The monastery was founded in the thirteenth century when a shepherd found a statue of the black virgin – La Moreneta – in woods nearby. According to lore she had a propensity for disappearing and reappearing again in the same spot she was originally found. After this happened several times, she was given a chapel of her own, the Basílica de la Mare de Déu de Lluc.

Ramon Llull's school

Llull believed that the monastery was situated on a sacred site and that the

magnetic properties of the earth were particularly strong here, making it an excellent place for study. He dabbled in all sorts of esoteric practices, but believed strongly in education for the masses. The boarding school that was later established on the site was long considered to offer one of the best educations in Spain.

Robert Graves' headstone

Nostra Senyora de Lluc monastery

WALK 7
Sóller and Port de Sóller

Sóller is one of the nicest towns on Mallorca, but lay relatively undiscovered until the road tunnel through the mountains to the town opened in 1997. It was one of the wealthiest places in Spain in the nineteenth century thanks to its citrus industry.

DISTANCE: 5km
TIME: A full day
START: Sóller
END: Port de Sóller
POINTS TO NOTE: Sóller is a fantastic alternative to Palma, and this walk assumes you will either be staying in the town or the port, or taking the delightful vintage train from Palma. A car is not necessary and there is a wide range of activities, ranging from soaking up the atmosphere of the Modernista town to hiking in the hills, to spending time on the beach at Port de Sóller. There is a reliable bus service that runs through other villages of the Serra de Tramuntana mountain range (www.tib.org) daily, which is convenient if you want to hook up with other walks in the area.

In the nineteenth century, Sóller not only produced large quantities of citrus fruits, but shipped them straight from the port to Marseille, generally bypassing Palma altogether – so the wealth generated stayed in this tiny enclave. Fast forward 100 or so years and the imposing Modernista mansions and smart plazas are, if anything, more manicured than ever, while the completion of a multimillion revamp of the Port de Sóller in mid-2011 gave the seafront a much-needed facelift. Today, both the inland town and the previously rather shabby port attract boutique hoteliers, fine restaurants and smart clubs, where discerning travellers – well-heeled 30-somethings as well as more mature couples – come to get away from it all in style.

If you are driving, leave Palma on highway Ma-11, following signs to Sóller. The journey takes only about 45 minutes, a far cry from the nine-hour trip along the old road, which cut over the **Coll de Sóller**, before the tunnel was built in 1997. Although famed for stunning views back to Palma, the old road was, and still is, vertiginous and slow going, with 28 hairpin bends on the way up and 30 more on the other side.

The Port de Sóller tram

Sóller

Even arriving in **Sóller** ❶ has a certain 'wow' factor, since the railway station has its own art gallery showing ceramics by Picasso and a handful of lithographs by Miró. It's not a bad way to start a mini-break in the country. The imposing peaks that surround the little town would give it an almost Alpine air were it not for the huge swathes of orange, almond and olive groves that surround it.

Follow the tram tracks down the hill a short distance to the light-dappled main square, **Plaça Constitució** ⓐ, dominated by the church of **Sant Bartomeu** ⓑ (free), its Modernista facade complemented by the ornate embellishments of the **Banco Santander** ⓒ bank on the opposite corner; both were the work of Joan Rubió, who was strongly influenced by Gaudí. The church, in fact, dates from the thirteenth century, although the main structure is seventeenth-century Baroque.

Carrer Sa Lluna

Leading off the square is **Carrer Sa Lluna** ⓓ, a pretty little street of honey-coloured stone with a handful of boutiques and art galleries for browsing. It was so named not because of the face of the moon carved into the side of the house at No. 50, but because of the way the moon comes up over the mountains at one end of it.

Also in Carrer Sa Lluna is another splendid and extremely colourful example of the Modernista style, **Can Prunera** ⓔ (www.canprunera.com; charge). This grand old townhouse, also the work of Joan Rubió, dates from 1911, and was a family home until 2006. It is a veritable jewel-box, featuring different, brightly patterned tiled floors, stained glass and an ostentatious spiral staircase rising up through the centre of the building. Many of the rooms, such as the dining room and some of the

The facade of Sant Bartomeu

Rustic apartments in Port de Sóller

The little vintage train

One of the most enjoyable excursions on Mallorca is to take the antique electric train from Palma to Sóller, which departs from the *fin-de-siècle* station in Palma's Plaça d'Espanya. It opened in 1912 and has been operating ever since – until the mid-1990s, it was the only comfortable way to get to Sóller. The scenery en route is lovely, especially in February and March when the almond blossom is in full bloom – a trip well worth making. Otherwise, you will shuffle your way through citrus groves and terraced hillsides until the train finally climbs over the mountains via a series of tunnels to descend into the orange-filled Sóller Valley.

Trains (www.trendesoller.com) leave Palma six times a day from Mar–Oct and four times a day from Nov–Feb and take about an hour to reach Sóller; bear in mind that train times vary depending on the season. The train makes a stop at Bunyola, from where it's a 35min-walk to the Jardínes de Alfàbia (www.jardines dealfabia.com; charge), one of Mallorca's most beautiful gardens, which dates back to Moorish times.

Catch the tram from Sóller to Port de Sóller

the work of a wide variety of local and international artists. There is an interesting sculpture garden at the back of the house too, and you could easily spend an hour or two here.

Sóller's other sights

Although Can Prunera is the main sight in town, it is well worth a stroll around to soak up the atmosphere and, if you're lucky, sneak a peek into the walled courtyards and gardens of the splendid old houses. Remember to look up under the eaves – many still exhibit old-fashioned painted roof tiles that depict farm scenes and other aspects of rural life. Now would also be a good time to stop for a glass of orange juice, for which the town is renowned, for an ice cream at the legendary

bedrooms, have been left decorated as they would have been during the Belle Epoque, but others have been given over to exhibition space for

Carrer Sa Lluna is a popular street for shopping

Hiking in Sóller

Sóller is probably the best base on the island for walkers, and the ingenious Associació Hotelera de Sóller (www.visitsoller.com) is a good way to go about it. With 26 hotels and hostels in their collection, they offer something for everyone and every budget, along with useful facilities ranging from detailed topographical maps to guided hiking trips from Feb–June and Sept–Oct (some of them free). Through the association you can also plan trips if you want to go it alone, or organise a guide to take you through the Tramuntana on a trip lasting several days. There are, however, plenty of easy half-day and day hikes that lead straight out of both the town and the port, which are well signposted and easy to follow. The variety of terrain is spectacular, ranging from ancient cobblestoned trails put in by the Moors to coastal walks where the reward at the end is a jump in the sea, to rolling farmland replete with fruit trees.

Sa Fàbrica de Gelats, see ①, or for something more substantial at the flamboyant **La Vila Hotel**, see ②, another Modernista gem, which serves an excellent lunch.

Museu Balear de Cienciès Naturals

On the western edge of town, the **Museu Balear de Cienciès Naturals** (www.museucienciesnaturals.org; charge) is a museum dedicated to promoting and preserving the natural assets of the island. The five exhibition rooms include collections of fossils, which are always popular with kids, as well as examples of indigenous flora and fauna. Also here is the **Jardí Botànic de Sóller**

Fresh oranges for sale   Al fresco dining in Sóller (www.jardibotanicdesoller.org; charge), which is strong on Balearic flora with some items from the Canaries and other Mediterranean islands too. This is a good place to start if you want to know more about what you are seeing when hiking.

A major festival

Sa Fira I Es Firó is a lively festival which takes place on the second weekend in May to celebrate Sóller's victory over the Moorish invaders on 11 May 1561. According to local lore, the town was saved by two '*valentes dones*' (brave women) who used the same bar they had barricaded their door with to kill their assailants, and successfully sent the corsairs packing. Big and little kids will be enthralled by the exciting battle re-enactments and spectacular evening firework display.

Port de Sóller

To get to the port, return to the town centre to catch the *tramvia* (tram) to **Port de Sóller ❷**. It leaves from both the railway station and the corner of the main square, stopping en route where requested; the journey takes about 20 minutes. The old-fashioned open-air wagons run on a line behind some of the village houses, allowing you to get a look at the small gardens, which adjoin virtually every house in Sóller, and you pass through orange and lemon groves and then travel

parallel to the main road before entering the little seaside town.

The port has undergone refurbishment and has a wider beach than before, as well as a prettified boardwalk skirting the entire length of the bay. The tram stops every 100m or so along the water's edge, allowing you to get off when you like. The first section – the **Plaça de la Torre** stop – is the best in terms of actual beach, a place to lay your towel and shallow waters in which to bathe. If you keep following the beach around to the left past the Platja d'en Repic, you'll eventually arrive at the **lighthouse**, which affords magnificent views over the bay. There is a simple restaurant at the hikers' **Refugi Muleta**, see ❸, or eat back on the beach at the **Hotel Marina**, which draws diners from near and far for its excellent paella - see ❹, an option for either lunch or dinner.

Santa Caterina

Continuing to the very last tram stop will bring you to the edge of the old fishermen's quarter – **Santa Caterina ❸**, always crowded with boats, some of which cruise (in the summer only) to the secluded Tramuntana beaches of Sa Calobra, Na Foradada and the Formentor peninsula. It is also a great place to eat, with several good fish and seafood restaurants.

If you clamber up through these narrow, winding streets you will eventually get to the **Església de**

View over the Port de Sóller

Food and Drink

1 Sa Fàbrica de Gelats

Plaça Mercat s/n;
www.gelatsoller.com; €.
No trip to Sóller would be considered
complete without stopping at this famous
ice-cream-making factory. This was
the first artisan *gelatería* on the island,
specialising in orange- and almond-
flavoured ice cream made from fruit and
nuts grown right here in the Sóller Valley.

2 La Vila Hotel

Plaça Constitució 14;
www.lavilahotel.com; €€
Although there is lots to be said for
sitting out on the plaza watching the
world go by, the real joy of eating at this
bijou hotel is the sheer magnificence of
its decor: all floral whimsy and naked
nymphs etched into pastel-coloured
stained glass. If you prefer to eat
alfresco there is also a secret garden
at the back when you can dine in the
shade of giant palm trees. Either way it's
widely considered to serve some of the
best modern Mallorcan cooking in town.

3 Refugi Muleta

Carretera Es Far de Cap
Gros s/n; tel: 971 634 271,
https://caminsdepedra.
conselldemallorca.cat/refugis; €
This is a popular stop for hikers
coming from Deià along the GR-221
trail, with stupendous views across
the Mediterranean, a picnic area
and the kind of hale and hearty fare
required after a morning of walking.
Think simple, traditional dishes at
wallet-friendly prices. Booking ahead
is advised, especially at weekends.

4 Hotel Marina

Platja d'en Repic s/n;
www.hotelmarinasoller.com; €€
Probably the most longstanding
hotel in the port, the Marina has
been run by the same family for four
generations. During all this time, one
of the highlights of eating here has
been the authentic seafood paella that
has people returning week after week
from as far away as Palma just to get
a taste of it. You can't beat eating at
a table on the beach-front terrace.

Santa Caterina (church) and the
attached Oratori de Santa Caterina
d'Alexandria (oratory), which
provides a fascinating glimpse into
the seafaring history of the town. In
years gone by it was a magnet for
pirates and corsairs, who were lured
like moths to a flame to the lucrative
little port. Even when the oratory
is closed, it is worth hiking up here
for the panoramic views, imagining
what it would have been like for
residents of old when ill winds blew
and their little town was in danger.

TOUR 8
Pollença and Formentor

The northernmost corner is a great spot for families. Spend time mooching about the pleasant market town of Pollença and its port, and enjoy the spectacular cliffs and quiet coves of the Formentor peninsula.

DISTANCE: 27km
TIME: A full day
START: Palma/Pollença
END: Pollença
POINTS TO NOTE: This tour assumes that you will be coming from Palma, although Pollença makes an excellent base for longer stays. The area has plenty of country villas to rent, complete with gardens and swimming pools – many of them more reasonably priced than you might expect – and many of the island's highlights, such as the west coast, Sóller and Palma, are less than an hour away. If you plan to do the tour in a day, Sunday sees Pollença at its liveliest, with lots of Mallorcan families enjoying their traditional lunchtime paella on the seafront in the port.

Getting to Pollença

From Palma, take the Ma-13 motorway to Inca, beyond which you turn left at the Crestatx junction, which puts you on the Ma-2220 straight to **Pollença ❶**. This is a pretty drive through rolling countryside, but avoids the twists and turns of the more dizzying Tramuntana roads.

The first sight you will see when coming into town is the hermitage of Nostra Senyora del Puig at 333m. There is, however, no road to the top so unless you fancy the strenuous hike, you might choose instead to go straight to the town centre. Park where you can and walk along the Via Pollentia to the main square to begin your tour.

Pollença

The central square, **Plaça Major ❹**, is where it all happens, with the tables of numerous bars and cafés spilling into it. It's lively in the evening with lots of people sitting outside to dine alfresco, while the surrounding side streets are good for boutique shopping.

But it is also a town that has several interesting sights. The fourteenth-century parish church on the square, **La Mare de Déu des Àngels ❸**, was built by the Knights Templar and is one of several religious buildings

Dining outside in Pollença

Pollença's galleries

The town's laid-back vibe has attracted numerous artists and it now has a handful of decent art galleries, among them the **Galería Dionís Bennàssar** **E** (Antoni Maura 11; www.galeriadionis bennassar.com), a nice contrast to the more figurative **Casa Museu Dionís Bennassar** **F** (Carrer Roca 14; www.museudionis bennassar.com), the home of the celebrated late local painter.

in the town, including the church of **Nostra Senyora del Roser**, as well as the **Sant Domingo** **C** and **Montesión**, all built in Baroque style.

El Calvarí

None, however, make their presence felt quite like the little chapel of **El Calvarí** **D**, home to a doll-like figure of Christ that makes an annual outing on Good Friday. The reason for its fame is not so much about Christianity as for the 365 steps that lead up to it, one for every day of the year. Should you be in town at Easter, the *Davallament*, or 'lowering' of Christ from his perch in the chapel of El Calvarí to the streets below, is an impressive spectacle and great fun.

Skirt the town centre by car to Carrer Huerto to pass the **Pont Romà** **G** en route to the port. The origins of the bridge are obscure, but it is thought to be part of the canal system built by the Romans in the second century AD.

Port de Pollença

The bay of Pollença is shaped like a lobster's claw, with **Port de Pollença** **2** situated right in the crook. It is lined with restaurants and hotels, many of which have been here since the resort's early days in the 1950s. Options range from **Stay**, see **1**, one of the finest restaurants in the upmarket marina, to **Bahia**, see **2**, for more traditional paellas and fish dishes.

El Calvarí steps

The Pont Romà

The resort is bookended by the **Punta de l'Avançada** to the West, which you can get to by walking along the pretty **Passeig d'es Pins** (Promenade of Pines), complete with numerous pocket-sized, sandy beaches and little jetties dotted along it – all ideal for small children.

The Formentor peninsula

The Carretera de Formentor runs parallel to the curve of the waterfront in the direction of the Formentor peninsula. You can join the Ma-2210 from it, and soon afterwards you will find yourself climbing quickly to the **Mirador des Colomer** ❸. The view down to the small island of El Colomer is simply stunning and one of

the most photographed on the island.

From here the road dips and ducks through rocky outcrops and pine forest, switching from one side of the peninsula to the other, providing spectacular views of the Bay of Pollença and the Mediterranean. Be warned that it is a bit gnarly, and tough going for anyone who suffers car sickness. It is worth the effort, though, especially if you keep left at the **Hotel Formentor** ❹, see ❸, and continue east through the woods towards the **Cap de Formentor** ❺, the northeastern tip of the island.

In the 1950s the Formentor Hotel was the place to see and be seen, and attracted a host of Hollywood A-listers such as Elizabeth Taylor, Audrey Hepburn and Charlie Chaplin, as

Breathtaking coastal road scenery

Food and Drink

1 Stay
Carrer Moll Nou s/n, Port de Pollença; www.stayrestaurant.com; €€€€
Offering more interesting dishes than many restaurants in the area, Stay is a popular choice for local foodies and visiting yachties. The terrace over the water and its location in the middle of the port give it an exclusive, romantic appeal.

2 Restaurante Bahia
Passeig Voramar s/n, Port de Pollença; www.hoposa.es; €€
With a terrace right on the sand, this is a perfect place for lunch if you're struggling to get the children off the beach. Simple grilled fish and rice dishes are the order of the day here, with some token grilled meat options available.

3 Hotel Formentor
Platja de Formentor 3; www.barcelo.com; €€€
If you are spending the day on the beach, the Formentor Hotel has a couple of options ranging from more formal restaurant dining to cheaper eats and child-friendly food at a beachside café. If you don't want to eat it's also a good place to sip a cocktail while you soak up the sun.

4 Lighthouse Café
Cap de Formentor s/n; tel: 619 748 591; €
A simple café serving basic snacks such as sandwiches and crisps, soft drinks, beer and coffee, and of course ice cream. It's not the sort of place you make a special trip for, but a fine stop-gap if you're out at the peninsula and need to refuel.

well as European luminaries like the infinitely tedious Duke of Windsor and Grace Kelly, who all came to relax here. The beach is wonderful, with fine, powdery sand draped with low-lying palm trees and gentle turquoise waters.

Capes and views
On the flat stretch you will pass the crumbling old houses of Cases Velles de Formentor, where one of Pollença's most famous citizens, the poet Costa i Llobera, spent much of his life, and way down below the road, only accessible on foot, is a rugged cove, **Cala Figuera 6**.

Continue through the tunnels to Formentor Lighthouse. The views out to sea here are tremendous. The first headland visible to the right (southeast) is **Cap des Pinar**, which divides the Badia de Pollença from the Badia d'Alcúdia. Beyond that is the peak of **Cap Ferrutx**, and further towards the horizon is the headland of **Cap des Freu**. There is a café at the lighthouse, see 4.

Sunrise at Formentor Lighthouse

TOUR 9
Bay of Alcúdia

The Bay of Alcúdia is Mallorca's most popular family resort and gets extremely busy in high season. With lots of watersports, it's great if you're travelling with teenagers and also has child-friendly hotels and restaurants. This tour also includes a couple of tips for getting off the beaten path.

> **DISTANCE:** 30km
> **TIME:** A full day
> **START:** Alcúdia
> **END:** Colònia de Sant Pere
> **POINTS TO NOTE:** The beaches hereabouts have plenty of family-oriented facilities, ranging from children's play parks to watersports outlets. The area also has several *ecovias* (bike paths) if you want to go on two wheels.

The great sweep of the Bay of Alcúdia offers everything you could need for a relaxed family holiday, while the ancient walled town of Alcúdia itself and the Parc Natural de S'Albufera both hold plenty of interest when you want to leave the beach behind.

Alcúdia

Alcúdia ❶ was originally the Roman town of Pollentia and it later became an important Moorish settlement (Al-Kudia meaning 'town on the hill'). A good chunk of the sturdy walls of the old *medina* (town) are still standing, and it is well worth a look around.

The road from Palma brings you along the Avinguda d'Inca; turn right at the roundabout next to the walls (signposted to Port d'Alcúdia), and follow it round to a car park on the left, close to the remains of the Roman city, the **Ciutat Romana de Pollentia**, which was excavated in the 1950s.

You can enter the old city here, straight onto the **Plaça de Jaume Qués Prevere ❹**. The Gothic church of Sant Jaume and a couple of small museums showing Roman and religious artefacts represent the bulk of the sights, but the main square, **Plaça Constitució ❽**, has some lovely Renaissance facades and good restaurants and cafés, and the little town is a pretty place for a stroll, especially if you are there for the Sunday or Tuesday morning markets, when you can shop for picnic food.

Alcúdia's old city walls

you aren't allowed to make the trip in a hire car. From here, follow signs to Can Picafort, which takes you out onto the bay road. You can also walk all the way from the port to Can Picafort on a modern boardwalk.

Platja d'Alcúdia

The Bay of Alcúdia is a 10km stretch of beach sheltered by low dunes. The first section of it, known simply as the **Platja d'Alcúdia 3**, is perfect for small children, offering abundant amenities, soft, powdery sand and shallow water. Its popularity means there's a good chance that children will find plenty of new friends to play with too.

Parc Natural de S'Albufera

About halfway between the port and Can Picafort you will find the **Parc Natural de S'Albufera 4** (www.balearsnatura.com; free), an 800-hectare (2,000-acre) expanse of lagoons and marshes that is one of the best birdwatching sites in the Balearics. It is particularly magical during the spring and autumn migration periods.

The road to Port d'Alcúdia

The road to the port is well signposted from the main town, and on the way there you may like to stop at the **Teatre Romà** (Roman Theatre). **Port d'Alcúdia 2** is not wildly interesting in its own right – and it is very touristy – but it's a good place to have lunch on the beach, such as at **Restaurant Miramar**, see **1**, and puts you at the start of the bay proper. It is also a convenient place to get a ferry across to Menorca, though

Shopping in Alcúdia

Ajuntament d'Alcúdia (town hall)

Watersports

The Bay of Alcúdia is a prime destination for water babies, with activities ranging from sailing and windsurfing to kayaking, water-skiing and scuba-diving. Many places are geared towards students, with courses ranging from a couple of hours up to a week. Most are open April–October.

Funny Beach Alcúdia, located on the beach at Alcudiamar, Ses Fotges and Alcúdia Pins (www.funnybeach alcudia.com) offers giant doughnuts, parasailing and banana flumes. Scuba Mallorca (Carrer d'Elcano 23, Port de Pollença; www.scuba mallorca.com) offers PADI courses for children and adults as well as equipment hire and/or dive trips for more experienced divers. Meanwhile, Watersports Mallorca (www.water sportsmallorca.com) has its main site on Playa de Muro offering windsurfing, kitesurfing, catamaran sailing and paddle boarding.

Platja de Muro

Sadly, much of the bay is heavily developed, though it is possible to find pockets of loveliness such as the **Platja de Muro ❺**. It's a bit wilder than the beaches closer to the port and is a great halfway house if you want amenities close by without the crowds. There are a handful of *chiringuitos* (beach bars, May–Sept only).

Food and Drink

❶ Restaurant Miramar

Passeig Marítim 2, Port d'Alcúdia; www.restaurantmiramar.es; €€€€
When a place has been around since 1871 you know it is doing something right, and this top-notch seafood restaurant in the otherwise touristy port is a gem. Service is excellent, views are fantastic, and the food is always fresh and locally sourced.

❷ Sa Xarxa

Passeig del Mar s/n, Colònia de Sant Pere; https://sa-xarxa.es; €€€
A laid-back terrace restaurant with fabulous views across the Bay of Alcúdia. Try homemade tapas including fried baby sardines and baby squid, or sea bass baked in salt with rosemary potatoes.

Colònia de Sant Pere

From Can Picafort the Ma-12 swings inwards, cutting out some of the seedier parts of the Bay of Alcúdia. Head back towards the coast just after Ses Pastoras on the Ma-3331, where you will see signs for the surfer spot of **Colònia de Sant Pere ❻** on the left. It provides a welcome antidote to the busy resorts, with its low-rise houses clustered around a small fishing port and a pebble beach. End your day with drinks and dinner at **Sa Xarxa**, see ❷.

Egrets in Parc Natural de S'Albufera

TOUR 10
Artà and Cala Torta

Mallorca has a beach for everyone, whether it's a secluded bay, a dune-backed shore or a surfer's hotspot. This itinerary is for serious beach-lovers combining some of the island's secret strands with an up-and-coming country town and lunch at a beach shack serving magnificent seafood.

DISTANCE: 19km
TIME: A full day
START/END: Artà
POINTS TO NOTE: A rental car is essential; there is no public transport to the remote beaches of the northeast. Try to catch Artà's lively Tuesday morning market and be aware that lunch at the beach hut depends on fair weather (they shut at the first sign of rain and all winter) – get there by 1pm for any hope of a table, as you can't book. It's also a tour better suited to early birds than those who like lazy mornings. Both the featured beaches are good for walking (one on sand, the other on cliff paths), so it can be done out of season. There are some memorable places to stay, such as Sa Duaia, Can Simoneta and Cases de Son Barbassa, but early booking is essential.

To get to Artà, take the Ma-15 from Palma to Manacor, and then continue northeast on the same road. It's a straightforward tour, clearly signposted all the way, although traffic can get heavy around Manacor, one of the island's main commercial hubs. Once you clear this, the scenery transforms into a series of low, gently undulating hills and lush agricultural land with the sea in the distance. Artà has lots going for it, ranging from stunning architecture to excellent local bistros and good shopping, but it seems it just hasn't been discovered yet by the masses.

Artà

Artà ❶ is hands down one of the loveliest towns on Mallorca, with handsome nineteenth-century townhouses, boutique shopping and an artsy community all watched over by the **Santuari de Sant Salvador d'Artà ❷** and surrounded by sturdy Moorish walls. It's worth the walk to get a bird's-eye view of the town, before spending a couple of hours exploring the backstreets in search of 'hippie-chic' clothing, designer interiors items and gourmet

Aerial view of Santuari de Sant Salvador d'Artà

picnic fare. It's also a great place to eat: try **Café Parisien**, see ❶. Once they've discovered it, people keep coming back, so if you want to stay here, book early.

A wild drive

One of the great joys of this tour is the drive itself, out across the headland that joins Cap de Ferrutx and the Cap des Freu. It's hard to imagine a terrain more different from that of the Tramuntana: wild and barren, windswept and remote.

Drive out of Artà in the direction of Capdepera and follow signs on the left just after the petrol station

to Cala Torta. This puts you on the bluff road that rises slowly upwards in a series of knobbly, windswept hills, more Atlantic than Mediterranean, the antithesis of the snug coves of much of the rest of the island, that gives an immense sense of freedom. There's even somewhere to stay – the romantic **Bar Restaurante Sa Duaia** (see page 91) which sits isolated among the hills – and from where there are several wonderful walks across the headland. If you keep going, within 10 minutes of the road starting its descent you come to lovely **Cala Torta** ❸.

The glorious bay of Cala Torta

Cala Torta

Popular among the surfing set, naturists and more independent travellers generally, Cala Torta is a scallop-shaped bay with cliff paths connecting it to other, still more secluded beaches. It's got a cool vibe, and the water is beautiful since it gets little by way of passing boats. There is no development whatsoever for miles. To the uninitiated it can seem a little brackish because of the sheer abundance of posidonia, a Mediterranean sea grass, but it's harmless, and indeed desirable since it prevents the beach from eroding. Unfortunately, it isn't entirely pleasing to the eye when there's a lot of it washed up on the beach, but you can always find a clear patch for getting in and out of the water, and it tends to remain in the shallows. Seclusion aside, the other reason for visiting Cala Torta is lunch. The eponymous bar, see ②, is nothing more than a wooden shack on stilts, but it serves some of the best grilled fish on the island.

Back to Artà

At the end of the day you have no option but to head back to Artà, but it's the perfect excuse to check out the bars and restaurants, some of which have live music in the evening. Café Parisien and Club Ca'n Moray are both good bets. Or head to Capdepera, which has a surprisingly lively scene for such a small place and some good

Food and Drink

① Café Parisien
Carrer Ciutat 18, Artà;
tel: 971 835 440; €€
Sitting here you could almost be in a bistro in Provence, offering Gallic and Italian-style dishes, jugs of fruity rosé and well-made cocktails. Nostalgic tunes take you back to another era, ranging from Bowie to live jazz bands throughout the summer, and it has a cosy, eclectic vibe that has you feeling like a local in no time.

② Bar Cala Torta
Platja Cala Torta s/n, Artà; €€€
With just four small tables on a tiny wooden deck, and a pint-sized kitchen at the back, this is arguably the smallest restaurant on Mallorca. Yet those in the know travel from far and wide to feast on simply grilled, spankingly fresh fish with crisp white wine to wash it down.

places to eat. Capdepera's main feature used to be its castle, which affords magnificent views of Menorca over to the east. Today, though, it is known for chic *agroturismos* and hip hotels. Capdepera is growing in popularity among more independent travellers. If you want to explore this part of the island the town is worth considering as an off-the-beaten-path base.

TOUR 11
Caves and Grottoes of the East

Mallorca has an extensive network of natural tunnels, caves and grottoes. Carved out by subterranean rivers over millennia, they resemble great man-made cathedrals and caverns and are simply jaw-dropping.

DISTANCE: 27km
TIME: A full day
START: Coves d'Artà
END: Coves d'es Hams
POINTS TO NOTE: Although this tour doesn't feature any beach time, it links nicely with tour 10 (Artà to Cala Torta) and works best if you visit one of the caves in the morning and hit the beach in the afternoon. Note that in high season traffic can be very heavy on the Ma-4023 which links the caves on this tour together.

The Jurassic limestone and karst formations that make up considerable chunks of the Balearic Islands are naturally porous. Indeed, neighbouring Menorca is nicknamed 'Swiss Cheese' among scuba-divers for its particularly porous coastal environs. Mallorca's best caves, by contrast, should be explored on foot, and currently there are six networks open to the public. The small but pretty grotto of Gènova, just outside Palma, is handy to have up your sleeve for a rainy day in the city, but to get to the serious stuff you need to head to the east of the island. This tour explores the best three examples of nature's architecture.

To get to the Coves d'Artà, drive east from Artà in the direction of Canyamel, bearing left at the Torre de Canyamel. This road leads you straight down to Cap Vermell and the caves.

The Coves d'Artà

The fact that the **Coves d'Artà** ❶ (Carretera de las Cuevas s/n; www.cuevasdearta.com; charge) are considerably less famous than their counterparts further south is a big part of their appeal: they are much quieter, especially if you time your visit out of season. Yet in some ways they are more spectacular. Less manicured than the prettified caves at Drach, the Coves d'Artà have a grisly history, which still permeates the atmosphere. Some 2,000 Moors hid in the caves after Jaume I's invasion of the island, but his Catalan troops smoked them out, then slaughtered everyone in one of the bloodiest massacres the island had ever seen. No one came back until the caves were 'rediscovered' in

Coves d'Artà

of purgatory'. Things lighten up a bit about halfway past the elephant formations and the 'Diamond Stones', but younger children can find it all a bit frightening. Tours last about 40 minutes. There are few facilities here, so pack snacks or head back out of town to the **Porxada de Sa Torre**, see ❶, located in an atmospheric thirteenth-century tower. Or, if you're looking for luxury, drive into Canyamel, which has the nicest beach in the area, and treat yourself to a lobster lunch at **Cap Vermell Grand Hotel Restaurant** see ❷, in a grand scenic location.

1876; they are now reputed to have been the inspiration for Jules Verne's *Journey to the Centre of the Earth*.

Visits are conducted in manageable groups, accompanied by rambunctious storytellers who paint a vivid scene. The first thing you'll see on entry is a gigantic stalagmite – 'The Queen of Columns' – rising 22m into the air. This is followed by the macabre additions of the 'chamber of hell' and the 'chamber

Porto Cristo

To get to **Porto Cristo** ❷, head back to the Ma-4040 and drive south to Son Severa, where a roundabout exit to the east puts you on the Ma-4023. This takes you straight into the town, the seat of Mallorca's only action during the Spanish Civil War, when a Republican battleship landed here with a force of 12,000. The troops managed to advance 10km inland,

The beach at Porto Cristo

Porto Colom

The less well-known little sister of Porto Cristo makes up in charm for what it lacks in size. Centred around two pocket-sized fishing ports, it's a lovely place to have lunch and spend an afternoon strolling along the shore and soaking up the atmosphere. If you can, try to catch it during the Mare de Déu del Carme festival on 16 June, when garlanded fishing boats head out to sea in a floating procession dedicated to their patron saint.

but the Nationalists soon drove them back, and life on the island remained predictably grim for any islander with Republican sympathies for the many decades of Franco's dictatorship.

A 1960s holiday resort

In its day, Porto Cristo was a popular holiday resort, although the centre seems a little jaded nowadays. Shops full of tourist tat and cafés selling chips have rather usurped the flavour of the place. However, it is pleasant enough and does retain a certain bucket-and-spade appeal. To get as much joy out of the place as possible, head down to the port on Carrer Burdils, which runs parallel to the beach, down the steps to the fishermen's quay and follow the edge of the inlet as it snakes into town. It's not Cala Figuera, but it's a pretty enough place to stretch your

legs, and there a couple of interesting architectural features to look at, such as the square at the intersection of Carrer del Mar and Carrer Sant Jordi (a good place to stop for a cup of coffee) and the church of Nostra Senyora del Carme in the square on Plaça del Carme.

The port and its environs are also your best bet for a quick bite, with plenty of places serving simple, family-friendly fare at reasonable prices, see **Sa Llonja** ③. If you're looking for something special you would be better off going down the coast a bit to Porto Colom or heading for one of the more rural restaurants inland. The area directly south of Porto Cristo boomed in the 1970s and today is almost completely lined with high-rise resorts. It does, however, have one redeeming feature: the excellent Roland (see page 100), widely considered to be one of the best restaurants on the island. For most people, though, the main reason to come to Porto Cristo is to enter the subterranean world of the **Coves del Drach** and the **Coves d'es Hams**.

Coves del Drach

The **Coves del Drach** ③ (Carretera Cuevas s/n; www.cuevasdeldrach.com; charge) to the south of town are Porto Cristo's main attraction, and understandably so. They have been tastefully lit to make the most of the intriguing journey that takes you nearly 2km underground, culminating in Europe's largest underground lake,

Porto Cristo's marina

Food and Drink

① Porxada de Sa Torre

Carretera Artà–Canyamel Km 5,
Capdepera; www.torredecanyamel.
com/es/gastronomia/
porxada-de-sa-torre; €€€
Decorated with ancient farming
implements, this place oozes character
from every inch of its historic stone
walls. The food is good, too, especially
the *lechon* (suckling pig) reared
on the restaurant's own farm and
slow cooked over an open fire, and
other traditional island dishes.

② Cap Vermell Grand Hotel Restaurant

Urb. Atalaya de , Canyamel;
www.capvermellgrandhotel.com; €€€€
Probably the best restaurant on this
stretch of coast, it forms part of a
smart hotel (see page 93) with a
magnificent terrace wedged between
the sea and the cliffs. Eat grilled
lobster fished from their own tanks,
or stop for a glass of champagne.

③ Sa Llonja

Passeig Moll 1, Porto Cristo;
tel: 971 822 859; €€€
Porto Cristo isn't the best place
on earth for food, but this port-
side restaurant is a good option.
Specialities include fresh seafood
as well as paella and other rice
dishes. There is a good wine list
and the place is child-friendly too.

where classical concerts are held and
pretty sloops, strung up with twinkling
lights, await to ferry you around.

It's all rather romantic in its whimsy,
and from the moment you enter
there is a certain magic in the air, for
these grottoes are straight out of fairy
tales, full of mysterious shapes and
formations, and weird and wonderful
colours. All in all, then, a carefully
staged experience, but one that has
earned itself the reputation of being
Mallorca's top sight. One word of
warning: these caves get unbelievably
busy and are best visited first thing in the
morning or last thing in the afternoon.

Coves d'es Hams

Alternatively you can visit
the **Coves d'es Hams ④**
(www.cuevasdelshams.com; charge),
which are about 1km north of
the town centre. These caves were
discovered by speleologist Pere
Caldentey in 1905 and feature more
of the same, albeit on a smaller scale,
complete with a subterranean lake
(called the Mar de Venecia) and
a floating concert platform, with
performances timed to coincide with
the tours. On your way to or from
the caves, consider stopping at the
charming inland town of Sant Llorenç.

Lighthouse in Porto Colom

TOUR 12
Es Trenc and the South

The flat, windswept landscape of the south makes it seem quite wild and isolated. Come here for bracing clifftop walks, to explore rural towns and pretty fishing villages, and to soak up the sun on secluded beaches.

DISTANCE: 29km

TIME: 2 days

START: Sa Ràpita

END: Cala Mondragó

POINTS TO NOTE: This tour is spread over two days. If you want to stay longer – and you might – there's plenty of great-value accommodation, especially around Santanyí, as well as some sweet if basic seaside hotels. If you don't have much time, choose sections of the tour such as an afternoon at Es Trenc or a morning at Santanyí market, and make it a day trip from Palma. A car is essential – there is little by way of public transport to these parts – and the tour is better suited to couples or young families looking for an alternative side to Mallorca than parents with teenagers looking for entertainment, or anyone wanting to party. It's a good tour to do at any time of the year if you're happy to swap sunbathing for rambling.

The quickest way to the south coast from Palma is to take the Ma-19 to Llucmajor, then the Ma-5040 to Campos. The Ma-6030 trunk road heads directly south, and from here the landscape opens out into a series of empty plains dotted with acacia and broom, twisted olive trees and almonds, with huge, piercing blue skies and almost no traffic. No wonder those who have discovered it have kept it to themselves – when you hear talk of 'another' Mallorca, look no further.

Sa Ràpita

This tour starts in the dusty backwater town of **Sa Ràpita** ❶, because although Es Trenc is the most famous beach in the Balearic Islands, it is curiously poorly signposted. The easiest option is to go to Sa Ràpita and walk along the beach from there, or to follow signs along a fairly rough A-road to **Ses Covetes** ❷, where there's a large car park, which places you handily about halfway along **Es Trenc** ❸ proper. The area is known for its salt production: Flor de Sal

Gleaming white sands at Es Trenc

d'Es Trenc (www.flordesal.com) does a range of gourmet salts including rose, black olive and Mediterranean herb, which are sold in delis and food shops all over the island.

Es Trenc beach

If Sa Ràpita is small and sleepy, with little going on beyond the remodelled marina, which does have a handful of good places to eat such as the **Club Nàutic La Ràpita**, see ❶, Es Trenc is a slice of old-fashioned beach paradise. With 3km of pristine white sand backed by low, tousled dunes, you could easily be fooled into thinking you're somewhere in the Hamptons, while the strong breezes that whip up can make it seem more

Atlantic than Mediterranean. Rest assured you are in the right place, as pools of turquoise merging with sapphire-blue waters attest. Eco-activists saved it from development back in the 1970s and ensured that the entire stretch got natural park status while keeping it fairly off-radar from many of the island's visitors.

Much of its appeal is the diversity that comes with the seasons: it is great for refreshing seaside walks if you come out of season, while the central section is beloved in the summer by nudists who seek shelter from the breeze in the dunes. The water is shallow enough for younger children to play safely, while teenagers and grown-ups romp around in the breakers when

Colònia de Sant Jordi

the wind gets up. You will find a real mix of ages, nationalities, couples and families here, all with one thing in common: a love of unspoilt beaches.

Happily, then, it is blessedly free of modern beach-going paraphernalia such as jet-skis, banana boats and other aquatic horrors. Facilities amount to a scant handful of *chiringuitos* (beach bars) dotted along its length, some of which rent sun loungers and Balinese-style grass parasols for the day, and serve basic lunches. The best is undoubtedly **Sa Copinya**, see ❷, and while you won't find Ibiza-style beach partying, it does have a lazy, laid-back vibe that keeps visitors coming back for more.

Colònia de Sant Jordi

From Sa Ràpita, drive back inland on the Ma-6030, turn right onto the Ma-6014, and then back down on the Ma-6040 to reach the settlement of **Colònia de Sant Jordi** ❹. Interest is growing in the place, mainly because it is from here that you catch the boat to the intriguing island of Cabrera (see page 73). **Colònia** was established in 1879 as a centre of agriculture and fishing, and it wasn't until the 1950s – as in the rest of the island – that tourists began to arrive. Even then it was a very slow trickle, and although increasing numbers of hotels, bars and restaurants have opened their doors in more recent years, it still has the thrill of a place less travelled.

Isla de Cabrera

Although it is no great beauty spot, it has plenty of rugged, seafaring character, and the seafront and port have been spruced up considerably in an attempt to attract the tourist euro. The shallow cliffs that separate the sea from the town make for a pleasant stroll before a lunch stop, maybe at **Port Blau** or **Es Punt**, see ❸ and ❹. If you are around during the first weekend of August, try to catch the annual Colònia de Sant Jordi summer festival, when you will find the streets overflowing with giant paellas, free-flowing beer and cava, and abundant music and dancing.

Secluded beaches

Colònia de Sant Jordi is also the place to head if you're inclined to seek out the island's more secluded beaches.

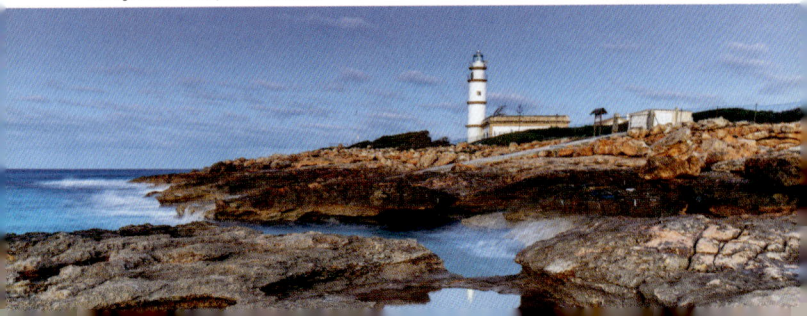

The lighthouse at Cap de Ses Salines

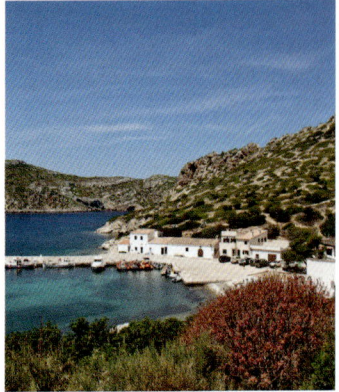

Heading east away from the town along the sand you will come to several scallop-shaped bays – Es Dolç, Els Estanys, Es Carbó, Ses Roquetes, Es Caragol – each more lovely than the last, and ultimately leading to **Cap de Ses Salines ❺**. It's a full day's walk to get there and back (you can also drive to the lighthouse from Ses Salines), but well worth the effort if you're seeking solitude. Do note, however, that there are no facilities en route.

Santanyí

Heading inland on the Ma-6100 from Colònia, you pass through the little town of **Ses Salines ❻**, which is good for a lunch stop at **Cassai**, see ❺, or a visit to **Botanicactus** (www.botanicactus.com), the largest cactus garden in Europe with more than 1,000 species from all over the world. Thereafter, you reach **Santanyí ❼**, which is the envy of other villages in Mallorca for its looks. The pinkish-hued stone used in the buildings here, besides being the most attractive of all of Mallorca's sandstones, is also the most durable and has been highly coveted at least since the Middle Ages, when it was used in such landmark buildings as Sa Llotja in Palma and the Castell Nuovo in Naples.

Today Santanyí is the loveliest town in the south, with a groovy, upwardly mobile vibe, thanks to the growing number of artists, writers and affluent second-home owners

Isla de Cabrera

Despite its diminutive size, 'Goat Island', as it is called in English, has a rather dramatic history, starting with the Napoleonic Wars, when it was used as a dumping ground for French prisoners, nearly two-thirds of whom died here. It was also a favoured hideout for the pirates and buccaneers who terrorised the neighbouring seas. These days it's an altogether more peaceful place. It was declared a national park in 1991, and nature-lovers will get a thrill from the sheer diversity of wildlife: there are seabirds aplenty, a chance of seeing dolphins playing in the surf, and an abundance of the rare Cabrera lizard. Once on terra firma after the boat ride, there is a castle, museum, lighthouse and caves to explore, as well as some cute little beaches for swimming and snorkelling. There is a small café on the island, but lunch can be provided on board the boat from Colònia de Sant Jordi, or you can take your own picnic. See www.excursionsacabrera.es for details.

moving in. It's a superb place to shop, with increasing numbers of boutiques selling high-quality goods like linen tablewear and delicate hand-painted ceramics, as well as several good art galleries, and a number of buzzy cafés and restaurants. One

Golden Barrel Cactus at Botanicactus garden, Ses Salines

Parc Natural de Mondragó

To the north of Cala Figuera, the wetlands and cliffs of the Parc Natural de Mondragó provide excellent birdwatching opportunities as well as some great walks and postcard-pretty beaches. It can be entered on both the south and north sides, although the south tends to be quieter. It was afforded national park status in 1992 and now comprises a couple of rocky, wooded headlands with lots of places for jumping into the sea and several picturesque beaches – S'Amarrador, Sa Font de n'Alís (where the information centre is located, and therefore the busiest) and the more secluded Caló des Burgit and Sa Barca Trencada – which all have varying degrees of amenities.

of the best is **Anoa Santanyí**, see ❻, praised as much for its friendly ambience as for its lovely food. Saturday is market day and it is well worth visiting specifically for this.

Nearby beaches

The nearest beaches are **Cala Llombards** ❽ and Cala Santanyí. The first is a narrow inlet sheltered by tall cliffs and pine trees, with golden sand and a casual, laid-back atmosphere that suits Santanyí down to the

ground. Throughout the summer sardines fresh off the boat are grilled over an open fire at a pop-up beach bar that also serves ice-cold beers to an appreciative crowd who sway to the sounds coming from the bar.

Cala Santanyí ❾ is more crowded because of the long-established Hotel Cala Santanyí (www.hotelcalasantanyi. com), which sits right on the beach. But that means there are better-organised facilities and a generally more family-oriented atmosphere.

Cala Figuera

From Santanyí it is a short distance to the picturesque harbour of **Cala Figuera** ❿, which wraps itself around the high, limestone cliffs here. The first recorded data of some kind of settlement here goes right back to 1306, although it didn't develop into a proper fishing village until the nineteenth century. Park at the top of town and walk down into the harbour, which is one of the unmissable sights on the south coast. Lined by ancient boathouses cut into the cliffs and by pretty, whitewashed fishermen's cottages trimmed with green, it absolutely oozes charm and is a delightful spot for a walk, especially if you arrive as the sun starts to go down, and perhaps before dining alfresco at one of the many restaurant terraces that look over its peaceful waters, such as **Restaurant es Port** (see page 101).

The picturesque town of Santanyí

Food and Drink

❶ Club Nàutic La Ràpita
Explanada del Puerto s/n, Sa Ràpita; www.clubnauticlarapita.com; €€€
This swanky-looking place stands alone at the end of the port, but don't be put off; the prices are more than reasonable and the terrace is one of the nicest on this stretch of coast, with excellent sea views. The cooking is likewise superb, offering delicious fresh fish and seafood, perfectly made paellas and service with a big smile.

❷ Sa Copinya
Platja de Ses Covetes s/n; €
Situated midway along Es Trenc (about 20 minutes' walk from Sa Ràpita), a more charming, low-key seaside shack you couldn't hope to find. Excellent fresh grilled sardines and succulent fried calamari served by barefoot waitresses add to the air of bonhomie.

❸ Port Blau
Carrer Gabriel Roca 67, Còlonia de Sant Jordi; www.portblau.es/en; €€€
This restaurant was opened by the Bauzà family back in 1965, and it continues to be a local favourite today. Buzzing with atmosphere, it's located right between the harbour and the beach and serves mainly Spanish seaside favourites like paella and *fideus*, as well as some child-friendly options.

❹ Es Punt
Avinguda de la Primavera 21, Còlonia de Sant Jordi; tel: 646 752 125; €€
This friendly local pub with a lively atmosphere is a great place to unwind with a few drinks after a day trip to the Isla Cabrera (they also have rooms if you want to stay the night). Food is basic, but most people come for the music – lots of funk, soul and occasional disco – making it the closest thing the town has to a nightclub.

❺ Cassai
Carrer Sitjar 5, Ses Salines; www.cassai.es; €€
A hip little restaurant with a focus on locally sourced, seasonal ingredients such as grilled cod with aioli, stone-seared duck breast and mountain lamb with herbs. It also does good afternoon teas, handy after brisk walks on the beach out of season.

❻ Anoa Santanyí
Carrer Aljub 32, Santanyí; www.anoa-santanyi.com; €€–€€€
Within walking distance from Plaça Mayor, this finely decorated restaurant caters mainly for German tourists. A simple menu includes exquisite Mallorcan and international dishes at reasonable prices. Try *sopa de pescado* (fish soup), pasta with prawns or veal steak. Professional and friendly staff.

Cala Figuera harbour

TOUR 13
Felanitx to Petra

This tour takes you into some of the most obscure parts of Mallorca's hinterland. Travelling the roads that connect the remote sanctuaries and monasteries scattered across the island, you'll cross the market gardens of the plains and ascend onto high plateaux, taking in orchards and olive groves bordered by ancient stone walls.

DISTANCE: 32km
TIME: A full day
START: Felanitx
END: Petra
POINTS TO NOTE: This tour can comfortably be done in a day. Should you wish to, however, you can stay overnight in either of the two former monasteries, both perched on hill-tops and with comfortably refurbished one-time monastic cells. It's a good Sunday tour that dips and weaves through one of the quietest, most agricultural parts of the island.

This tour will take you through parts of the island that many visitors do not see, where the beauty of the scenery is complemented by the peaceful nature of villages that time seems to have forgotten. The monasteries themselves are oases of calm, and if you have the time and inclination to stay overnight in one of them, it will be an unforgettable experience.

Felanitx to Santuari de Sant Salvador

Felanitx ❶ is not a wildly interesting town in its own right, although the church of Sant Miquel is impressive and there is a good Sunday market that is particularly strong in terms of local produce. It is also proud to be the birthplace of the artist Miquel Barceló, who had his first exhibition at La Caixa bank here in 1972. His work was immediately coveted and he quickly began to show in other towns across Mallorca and the rest of the world. In 2007 he decorated the chapel of St Peter in Palma's cathedral which portrays, in ceramic clay, the feeding of the 5,000 and the miracle of the loaves and fishes. Fiercely proud of his homeland, in

Sant Miquel church

2013 Barceló did an audio-visual presentation and designed the logo for Mallorca Blackout (www.gob mallorca.com), an environmental campaign to stop further over-development of the island.

Traditionally, the town has long been known for its wine and brandy, and it remains largely agricultural today, pleasingly devoid of the usual trappings of tourism. If you do stop here, keep an eye out for traditional terracotta water-coolers, which have been made in Felanitx for millennia.

At 516m, the **Santuari de Sant Salvador** ❷ sits at the highest point of the south of the island and straddles two horn-shaped peaks. The higher is occupied by a fourteenth-century fortress, which alas is closed to the public, whilst the lower part holds an ancient monastery that has been turned into a charming hotel and restaurant (www.santsalvadorhotel.com). It's a rewarding, if steep walk (about 3km) between the two: a good way to blow away the cobwebs and a great place for landscape photographers to capture the shimmering early morning light.

Once back in Felanitx, head

Giant sculptures at Paprika fair

Santuari de Sant Salvador

north-west on the Ma-5100 in the direction of the small town of **Porreres** ❸. Just outside is the tiny **Santuari de Monti-Sion** ❹, worth a stop if you really want to take the sanctuary theme to extremes – but it's recommended here mainly as a place to stop for a picnic, although it's worth building an appetite for a heartier lunch at **L'Escrivania**, see ❶, before continuing on your way.

Santuari de Cura

From Porreres take the Ma-5030 to the Ma-15 motorway, turning left shortly after to join the picturesque Ma-5017 road, following signs for the sleepy, picturesque village of **Randa** ❺, which is said to be one of the prettiest villages on the island. The road snakes its way through the village and up to the tabletop mountain of **Puig de Randa**, passing stone cottages with pretty, moss-green shutters tumbling over with bright blooms, while tinkling streams go gurgling through. On top of the *puig* (mountain) is the **Santuari de Cura** ❻, a handsome former monastery where the scholar and missionary Ramon Llull set up a retreat and centre for learning in the thirteenth century.

Ramon Llull's centre of learning

The sanctuary didn't become a full-blown monastery until the seventeenth century, and even now it oozes a certain scholastic air. Today it encompasses a small chapel, pretty gardens and a museum dedicated to the life and works of Llull: **Museu del Aula de Gramática Ramón Llull**. There is also a café-cum-restaurant. Most visitors just come to admire the views, but you could spend the night (www.santuaridecura.com) if you so desired. There are three oratories on the way up the hill, and, down below in the village, **Es Recó de Randa** is a good stop for food, see ❷.

Petra

Continuing along the Ma-15, the road sweeps northeast through the pleasing little towns of Montuiri and Sant Joan to **Petra** ❼, a formerly a dusty country town in the middle of nowhere, but now much more lively and appealing. Both Petra's church and its museum, the **Casa Museu Fra Juníper Serra** (www.illesbalears. travel/en/mallorca/museum-casa-de-junipero-serra-cal-pare-serra) are worth a look, but mainly to enjoy the pretty garden and as a means of placing the history of Fray Junipero Serra (1713–84) in context.

This Franciscan monk was Mallorca's most famous missionary, and one of the island's best-known sons. The fruits of his colonial labours are particularly prevalent in parts of California, where he founded a number of

Lunching at the Santuari de Cura

Food and Drink

1 L'Escrivania

Plaça de la Vila 1, Porreres;
www.lescrivaniarestaurant.com; €€
Atmospheric restaurant in what
was once the town hall. Tasty
lunches and dinners with local,
seasonal ingredients to the fore.

2 Es Recó de Randa

Carrer Font 21, Randa;
www.hotelesrecoderanda.
com-hotel.com/en/; €€
A pretty, seventeenth-century inn
that is especially good on a chilly
day in winter, when they light the
fire in the dining room. Expect to
find hearty country classics such
as wood-roasted suckling pig
and *arroz brut* (clay-pot rice).

3 Dolc y Dolc

Carrer Sol 53, Petra; tel: 971 830 036; €
In the centre of town, this good
pizzeria also does delicious salads,
baguettes and desserts – try the
blueberry cheesecake. It is super-
friendly and serves enormous
portions. It's a great place to come
after a long day's sightseeing or
walking, but be warned that you want
to come here really hungry. Excellent
value and a nice outdoor terrace.

missions, including the one that is now the city of San Francisco.

Eating in Petra

It is the town itself that is the best place to spend a couple of hours and a great spot for foodies, with several excellent places to eat, as well as its own local winery, the **Bodega Miquel Olivera** (Carrer Font 26; www.miqueloliver.com), which has excellent fruity wines made by one of the island's few female wine-makers, Pilar Oliver.

If you are having lunch in Petra, or staying for dinner, **Dolc y Dolc** is highly recommended, see 3. Petra is one of the top spots on the island for *cuina Mallorquina*, traditional country cooking, particularly at its cool and cavernous *cellers* – old-fashioned bodegas.

Sineu Market

A short detour from Petra along the Ma-3330 takes you to **Sineu**, an agricultural village, which on Wednesdays boasts the oldest market on the island. Dating back to 1306, it is the only one that still deals in livestock and is also a good place to pick up foodie gifts and high-quality crafts. Other than that, the main sight in town is the medieval church, Nostra Senyora dels Àngels. Stop for a coffee in Café Sa Plaça in the main square before heading off.

Religious manuscripts in Petra

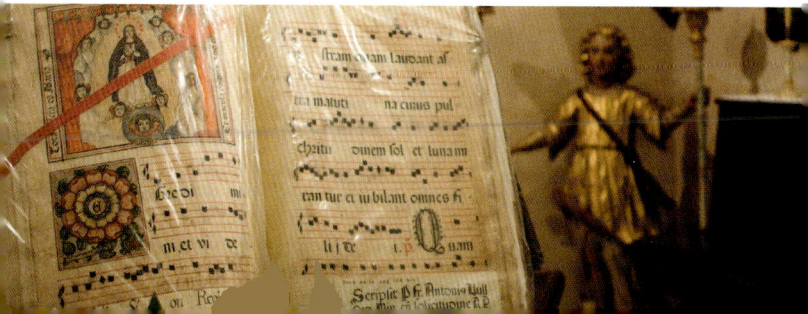

TOUR 14
Wine Country

Mallorca has made its mark as a serious winemaking region, much of it centred around the rural town of Binissalem, a good base for visiting some of the best and most exciting wineries and getting to grips with the endemic grape varieties while doing some pleasant sipping and swirling.

DISTANCE: 25km
TIME: A full day
START: Santa Maria del Camí
END: Binissalem
POINTS TO NOTE: This tour is created for driving, but it could easily be done by bicycle since distances are short and the region is flat. The best time of year to do it is September, when the grape harvest celebrations take place, but if you find yourself here in August, the Bodega Vins Nadal hosts a super jazz festival. With a dozen or so different wineries – details of which can be seen at www.binissalemdo.com – now open to the public, you could easily make the tour last a few days or a long weekend. This tour takes in a broad selection to serve as a general introduction to the area.

Wine has been made on Mallorca since Roman times, and the vintages were highly regarded, too, compared by the historian Pliny to the finest wines in Italy. Over time the production of wine spread across the island into the regions of Bunyola, Campos, Felanitx, Manacor, Porreres and Valldemossa, although much of it was wiped out during the phylloxera outbreak in the 1890s. Up until this point, and unlike the rest of Europe, the island had remained blessedly free of the wine louse, but in the following 100 years production fell from 30,000 hectares (75,000 acres) to a mere 2,000 (5,000). It wasn't until the 1960s that wine production started up in earnest again, and as interest in Spain as a gourmet destination grew in the mid-1990s, so winemakers in Mallorca upped their game. Today they offer some of the most exciting (and expensive) wines in the country, and there is no better place to get acquainted with them. The most important local grape varieties are Manto Negro, Callet and Moll (red) and Premsal Blanco (white). Look out for these on the bottle labels to get a proper taste of Mallorca's distinctive *terroir*.

Santa Maria del Camí
Away from the coasts, the quiet

Village of Santa Maria del Camí

countryside and ancient towns of the Mallorcan interior have remained largely unaffected by tourism, offering a taste of old-style island life to those who make the effort to go and find it. Take the Ma-13 highway from Palma in the direction of Inca, and within 15 minutes you will see signs to the pretty village of **Santa Maria del Camí** ❶ – a good place to fuel up with a strong cup of coffee in the main square before this tour begins.

Macià Batle ❷ (Camí de Coanegra s/n, Santa Maria del Camí; www.macia batle.com; guided visits) is located just a little way north of the town centre, and is one of Mallorca's best-known

wineries, occupying an impressive position on the plains, with the Tramuntana mountain range rising up behind. The winery is well geared for visits, with a smart tasting room that looks out over the maceration tanks and the vineyards, but the labels themselves are also noteworthy, as each has been designed by a famous artist – both international names and local: among them are Rebecca Horn, Yannick Vu and Pep Coll. At the other end of the scale, **Celler Sebastià Pastor** ❸ (Carrer Paborde Jaume 17, Santa Maria del Camí; www.sebastiapastor.com) is a far more modest affair, but interesting because here they make wines using

The perfect setting for wine tasting

Celler restaurants

Most of what you read about Inca is in the context of its leather-working past and its current incarnation as a shoe manufacturing centre. Nevertheless, Inca is, in fact, far more interesting as the centre of centuries-old wine *cellers*, which operated much like modern-day wine bars. Most didn't start serving food until the mid-twentieth century, but once they did, a whole new tradition of *celler* cuisine was born: one that was hale and hearty, featuring local produce in abundance, and restored regional recipes such as roast quail and pork wrapped in cabbage leaves to their place at the top of the island's culinary hierarchy. Come to Inca to eat rather than shop, and you won't leave disappointed.

only local grape varieties. The wine is simple – table wines rather than great vintages – but an enjoyable variety that is perfect for picnics. If you are in the area at lunchtime, it's worth making a short detour northwest for lunch at the delightful **Moli des Torrent**, see ❶.

Sencelles

On the road to Sencelles you will pass **Bodegas Angel** ❹ (Carretera Santa Maria–Sencelles Km 4.8; www.bodegasangel.com), one of the most state-of-the art, modern wineries

on the island, which prides itself on excellent new-wave wines, including a stupendous white. For anyone who appreciates small-production boutique wines, this is one not to be missed.

Continue in the direction of the one-horse town of **Sencelles** ❺ and just outside you will find **Ca Sa Padrina** ❻ (Cami dels Horts s/n, Sencelles; tel: 660 211 939 or 646 318 600; http://vinscasapadrina.com; phone in advance to arrange a visit), which is likewise intent on rediscovering traditional winemaking techniques by using only endemic grape varieties and harvesting everything by hand. Again, it's a must for serious wine drinkers.

A traditional winery

Heading directly north out of Sencelles, **Can Remis** ❼ (Carrer Sor Francinaina Ana Cirer 14, Sencelles; https://canramis.com) is one of the oldest wineries and brandy distillers on the island, dating back to 1870. It makes a striking contrast to the more contemporary facilities you will have visited earlier in the day, and is a good halfway point for breaking for lunch.

Binissalem

If you are happy to keep going, continue north to **Binissalem** ❽, which has several good eating options and puts you at the heart of wine-growing country. But be sure to save enough energy to stop en route at the **Bodega Biniagual** ❾ (Ap. Correos 5; tel: 971

Wine vats

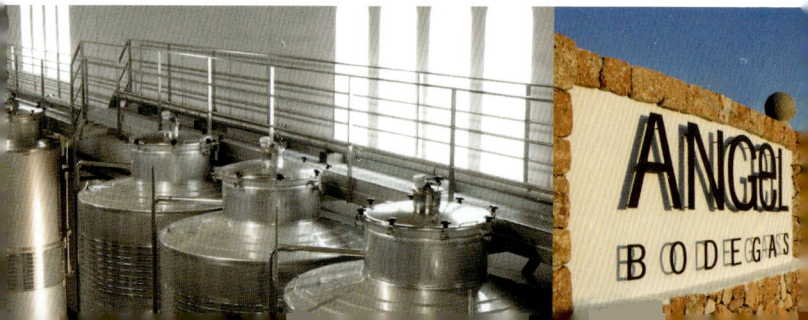

870 111; www.finca-biniagual.com; phone ahead to arrange a visit), arguably the prettiest winery on the island. The cooperative occupies the whole hamlet of Biniagual and attracts some of Spain's most talented winemakers, so it always makes for interesting drinking. They also produce olive oil.

Just before you reach **Binissalem**, **Bodegas Antonio Nadal** ⑩ (Finca Son Roig, Camí de Son Roig, Binissalem; www.antonionadalros. com) was the first winery on the island to gain D.O. status back in 1989. Its wines are still considered to be among the best, and if you treat yourself to a bottle of Magdalena Nadal Estela you will find out why.

And so to Binissalem, the official seat of the D.O. (Denominación de Origen). Vins Nadal (Carrer Ramon Llull 2, Binissalem; www.vinsnadal.es/en/) offers consistently high-quality wines at reasonable prices. They also stage jazz concerts in the cellars in the summer, combining great food, wine and music. It's well worth bagging a ticket for these if you can (see the website for details). But no visit is complete without stopping at José Luis Ferrer (Carrer Conquistador 103; www.vinosferrer. com), probably the island's most famous winery. The distinctive orange label of their crianza is the house wine of choice for restaurants all over Mallorca.

There are several good places to eat in or near Binissalem. End the day either with a full dinner or drinks on the square: in town, try **Can Jan** or venture over to Sencelles for **Sa Cuina de N'aina**, see ② and ③.

Food and Drink

① Moli des Torrent
Carreterade Bunyola (Ma-2020), Santa Maria del Camí; www.molidestorrent.de; €€€
On the western outskirts of town, this beautiful, restored windmill is a lovely place to dine alfresco in the summer and well worth the detour. The German-run restaurant focuses on seasonal regional cuisine and features the likes of prawns with potato salad followed by apple strudel. There is a good selection of Mallorcan wines and also German beers.

② Can Jan
Plaça de l'Església 5, Binissalem www.canjan.es; €€.
Cosy and informal little place where the home cooking is tasty and substantial.

③ Sa Cuina de N'aina
Carrer Rafal 31, Sencelles; www.sacuinadenaina.com; €€
Family-run small restaurant set around an attractive interior courtyard. The food, like the surroundings, is traditional: roast suckling pig and lamb are the house specialities. Home-made fig ice cream is a winner for dessert.

Entrance to the winery

Grapes at Bodegas Angel

DIRECTORY

Our edit of the best hotels, restaurants and evening entertainment to suit all tastes and budgets, plus an A–Z of all the essential information you need to know, a quick language guide, and some great book and film recommendations to give you a flavour of Mallorca.

Accommodation

Mallorca has a wide range of accommodation, ranging from trendy boutiques in Palma to chic farmhouse accommodation inland. Hotels are rated from one to five stars but bear in mind that the rating is related to the facilities offered and not the quality of service.

Small family-run establishments in the lower categories can be more comfortable than large resort hotels: try **Little Hotels** (www.littlehotels. co.uk) and **Secret Places** (www.secret places.com). For rural hotels, villas and apartments see **Rural Hotels Mallorca** (www.ruralhotelsmallorca. com). Most deluxe accommodation is clustered around the west coast, while you can get great package deals if you head east. Some hotels close for a few months off season, but those that remain open tend to have good offers. This list only covers areas included in the walks and tours, and some areas are stronger than others in terms of places to stay. The Bay of Alcúdia, for example, caters mainly for package tourists, so we recommend staying in nearby Pollença if you want a different experience.

The following guide indicates prices for a standard double room in high season, but should be used as an approximate guide only. VAT (IVA) at 10 percent and breakfast are sometimes

Accommodation Price Code

Price for a double room for one night in high season:
€€€€ = above 250 euros
€€€ = 150–250 euros
€€ = 120–150 euros
€ = below 120 euros

included in a quoted rate, but it is wise to check. Prices do not include the eco-tax introduced in 2016, applying to visitors and residents over 16 (costing up to €4 a night in high season).

Walkers will find plenty of basic refuges and hostels, but campsites are few and far between. Those seeking peace and quiet should consider staying in a monastery, especially Lluc.

Palma

Hotel Almudaina
Avinguda Jaume III 9;
www.hotelalmudaina.com; €€€
Comfortable and moderately priced with obliging staff, the Almudaina is on Palma's foremost shopping street. Established in 1972, it was completely renovated 20 years later. There are magnificent views across the city and bay from the terrace, bar and upper-floor rooms.

Hotel Bon Sol's opulent lobby

Hotel Bon Sol
Passeig de Illetes 30; www.hotelbonsol.es; €€€
This quirky family-run hotel is a
delight, about a 20-minute taxi
ride (or bus trip) from the centre.
Heavy Spanish furnishings in the
lobby are complemented by light,
airy bedrooms; gardens and terraces
cascade down to the sea; and there's
a private beach. Yoga classes and spa
facilities are included in the price.

Hotel Born
Carrer Sant Jaume 3;
www.hotelborn.com; €€€
A taste of the Palma that was, this
lovingly renovated mansion is right
in the heart of the city and oozes
atmosphere, though some rooms
are showing their age. Regardless,
it's spotlessly clean and the open-
air courtyard where breakfast
is served is hard to beat.

Hotel Convent de la Missió
Carrer de la Missió 7;
www.conventdelamissio.com; €€€
This stylish hotel, set in a converted
seventeenth-century convent in the old
quarter, has minimalist all-white rooms,
a roof terrace, solarium and steam
rooms, and an excellent restaurant, Marc
Fosh. The art gallery, housed in the old
refectory, hosts temporary exhibitions

Hotel Feliz
Avinguda de Joan Miró 74;
www.hotelfeliz.com; €€€

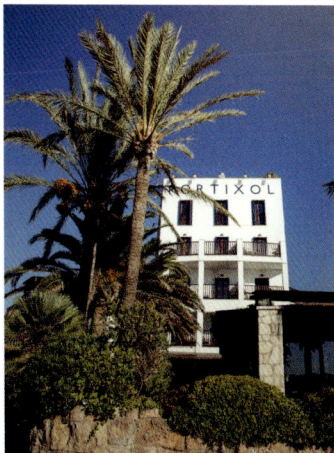

Hotel Portixol

Feliz has a Scandinavian aesthetic
boosted by lots of bright colour woven
into an old 1960s apartment block.
The 'fish tank' swimming pool on
the terrace is fun, while the ample
lounge – stuffed with squishy sofas –
is a great place to chill out at night.

Hotel Portixol
Carrer Sirena 27, Portixol;
www.portixol.com; €€€€
The hotel of choice for hip young
things wanting to hang out on the
beach, Portixol ticks a lot of boxes:
chichi lounge and cocktail bar, great
food, a pool to be seen in, plentiful
pampering treatments. The seafaring
theme in the bedrooms extends to
binoculars for watching the wildlife.

Room at the Palacio Ca Sa Galesa

Self-consciously stylish hotel, Puro has designer chic emanating from every faux animal skin-covered pouf or sleek leather armchair. It pays to be a creature of the night when staying here – it's somewhere to party rather than chill out. The hotel also has a tasteful beach club just beyond Ciutat Jardi.

Hotel San Lorenzo
Carrer San Lorenzo 14; www.hotelsanlorenzo.com; €€€
This enchanting little hotel (only nine rooms) is nearly always booked well in advance. The bright rooms are individually decorated in traditional Mallorcan style; all have balconies, and some have garden access. If you don't fancy heading to the beach there is a small pool.

Palacio Ca Sa Galesa
Carrer Miramar 8; www.palaciocasagalesa.com; €€€€
Housed in a grand, meticulously restored seventeenth-century palace, this tiny hotel (only 12 rooms) is furnished with antiques, has a courtyard with fountain, and an indoor pool.

Hotel Tres
Carrer Apuntadors 3; www.hoteltres.com; €€€€
A sleek, contemporary renovation of an aristocratic townhouse, Tres attracts a more grown-up crowd than Puro, without being stuffy. Rooms are stylish and spacious, the central courtyard and lounge are both great places for breakfast and hanging out, and two roof terraces give splendid city views.

Palau Sa Font
Carrer Apuntadors 38; www.palausafont.com; €€€
A delightful hotel in a sixteenth-century episcopal palace, with 19 individually decorated rooms – those at the back are quieter, but this is the quiet end of the busy street. Buffet breakfast included.

Andratx to Banyalbufar
Hotel Brismar
Almirante Riera Alemany 6, Port d'Andratx; www.hotelbrismar.com; €€
This comfortable and simple seafront hotel is a bargain given the coveted location. Ask for a room with a view

Puro Hotel
Carrer Montenegro 12; www.purohotel.com; €€€€

Jumeirah Port Sóller hotel and spa

of the harbour, although these are the noisiest. The restaurant serves traditional Mallorcan food and has lovely views across the port.

L'Escaleta
Carrer del Porvenir 10, S'Arracó; www.hotelescaleta.com; €€

Attractively converted old schoolhouse located a short distance inland from Sant Elm. Rooms are individually furnished in traditional style, plus there is a pool and a lovely garden where dinner is served on some evenings by prior arrangement. Ideal for hikers and cyclists. Breakfast included.

Finca S'Olivar
Carretera Ma-10 Km 93.5, Estellencs; www.fincaolivar.org; €€

Gorgeous *agroturisme* set in a 15-acre private valley with wonderful views over the coast. The self-catering accommodation (breakfast available) is in two traditional stone houses and two cottages. There is an idyllic infinity pool with a terrace.

Hotel Mar-i-Vent
Carrer Major 49, Banyalbufar; www.hotelmarivent.com; €€€

This family-run hotel was one of the original hotels to spring up on the west coast. The bedrooms are light and airy if fairly basic, but the main reason to stay here is to take advantage of its extraordinary clifftop pool and dazzling sea views.

Hotel Rural Nord
Plaça d'es Triquet 4, Estellencs; www.hotelruralnord.com; €€

This traditional stone village house is built around a courtyard that has been revamped with a designer's touch. Sunny bedrooms, local produce and a restored olive mill for drinks at the end of the day deliver far more than you would expect from the price tag. A real bargain.

Villages of the Tramuntana
Hotel Son Palou
Plaça de la Església s/n, Orient; www.sonpalou.com; €€€

Tranquil, beautiful and stylish, Son Palou is regularly voted best base on the island by hikers, so book well in advance if you want to stay here. It has cosy lounges (complete with crackling fires in winter), romantic bedrooms, rambling gardens, a huge pool and a superb restaurant specialising in traditional country cooking.

Valldemossa to Lluc
(A Belmond Hotel) La Residencia
Son Moragues, Deià; www.belmond. com/la-residencia-mallorca/; €€€€

Probably Mallorca's most famous hotel, La Residencia is loved by visiting celebrities and European glitterati. Set in two chic and elegant sixteenth-century manor houses, this is the place to be if you value privacy and a hotel capable of satisfying your every whim – no matter how excessive.

The modern Mallorcan restaurant El Olivo is highly regarded.

Es Molí
Carretera Valldemossa–Deià s/n;
www.esmoli.com; €€€€

Es Molí is a magical place occupying several acres of lush gardens at the foot of Es Teix mountain, overlooking the sea. It has a contemporary feel, personal service and romantic ambience. Access to a private beach – Sa Muleta – is an added bonus.

Pension Miramar
Carrer Ca'n Oliver s/n, Deià;
http://pensionmiramardeia.com; €€

Set above the main road up a narrow lane, this pleasant little *hostal* has a cavernous entrance hall and nine rooms (not all have bathrooms). Breakfast, which is included in the price, is served on the terrace. The walls are adorned with works by artists who have stayed there over the years.

Sóller and Port de Sóller

L'Avenida
Gran Via 9, Sóller;
www.avenida-hotel.com; €€€€

One of the hippest boutiques on the island, L'Avenida has just 12 luxury suites, each more glamorous than the last. Elsewhere, communal areas are dripping in luxury, while the arcaded terraces around the pool are the height of sophisticated elegance. This place is fantastic for romantic weekend getaways.

Hotel Esplendido
Es Traves s/n, Port de Sóller;
www.esplendidohotel.com; €€€€

The grooviest hotel on the Port de Sóller seafront, Esplendido is owned by the same people as the Portixol in Palma and despite its size, it has a boutique appeal. Surrounded by the beautiful Tramuntana mountains, it's the perfect place to relax, especially in the spa. The hotel has firmly established itself as the place *du jour* among style-savvy travellers.

Jumeirah Port Sóller Hotel & Spa
Carrer Belgica s/n;
www.jumeirah.com; €€€€

This dazzling five-star hotel has been described as one of the finest in the Mediterranean. With stunning cliff-top views, two gourmet restaurants, four bars, two swimming pools and a spa, you won't be searching for things to do. It is, perhaps, a little too grand for its own good – the architecture is so modern that getting lost seems easy.

Es Port
Carrer Antonio Montis s/n, Port de Sóller;
www.hotelesport.com; €€€

This meticulously restored and enlarged old stone farmhouse is hugely popular with hikers. With several living rooms built around an ancient olive press, rambling gardens, two huge pools (outdoor and in) and crackling fires in the winter, you can see why so many people keep coming back for more.

Inside La Residencia

Pollença and Fortmentor

Hostal Bahia

Passeig Voramar s/n, Port de
Pollença; www.hoposa.es; €€€

An attractive and friendly
establishment in a nineteenth-
century summer villa, with an
inviting terrace, right by the sea.

Hotel Formentor

Platja de Formentor s/n, Formentor;
www.mallorcaformentor.com/en/; €€€€

Overlooking the beach and with
amazing gardens, this classic hotel
has been around since the 1950s,
when it was something of a haven
for travelling stars; Ava Gardener
and Elizabeth Taylor both stayed
here. Since those heady days, the
hotel has had more downs than
ups, but is now in the competent
hands of the Four Seasons chain.

L'Hostal Pollença

Carrer Mercat 18, Pollença;
www.pollensahotels.com; €€

This place is excellent value for money:
it's really a B&B that's gone upmarket,
with a lively ambience, colourful rooms
all with en suite bathrooms, and a
groovy retro public room for trading
books and gossiping. Breakfast is served
at the sister-hotel around the corner,
the Hotel Juma on the main square.

Son Brull

Carretera Palma–Pollenfa Km 49.8,
Pollença; www.sonbrull.com; €€€€

The view from Hotel Formentor

One of the most stylish boutique
hotels on the island, Son Brull is a
monastery that has been converted into
a shrine to contemporary minimalism.
Perfect for design aficionados, yet
unexpectedly welcoming to children;
expect lots of clean lines, futuristic
food and impeccable service.

Artà and Cala Torta

Sa Duaía

Carretera Artà–Cala Torta Km 8;
www.saduaia.com; €€

A secret hideaway on the bluff above
Artà, this place attracts an alternative
crowd who enjoy a bit of splendid
isolation. Apartments are rustic but
comfortable, it has a great pool, and

Son Brull hotel

This chic rural retreat is like the new-wave *agroturismos* of Ibiza: a collection of spacious suites built of stone and wood spread across several olive groves, a pool area surrounded by draped day beds, fantastic food and the sensation that you're miles from anywhere. Breakfast is included.

Hoposa Niu
Carrer Cala Barques s/n, Cala San Vicenç; www.hoposa.es; €€€
This pleasant, owner-managed hotel overlooking the lovely cove of Cala Sant Vicenç has facilities including terraces, a bar and an excellent restaurant specialising in fish and lobster. Reserve well in advance.

Caves and Grottoes of the East
Can Simoneta
Carretera Artà–Canyamel Km 8, Capdepera; www.cansimoneta.com; €€€€
A spectacularly located boutique hotel occupying several acres of cliff-top above the sea. Inside, think cool minimalism, outside manicured lawns, hammocks and a staircase to a private beach. With just eight rooms, service is highly personalised – perfect for a romantic getaway or honeymoon. Breakfast included.

Hostal Porto Colom
Carrer Cristófol Colom 5, Porto Colom; www.hostalportocolom.com; €€
Situated right by the port, this pleasant, one-star hotel in an ochre-

though the food is fairly ordinary, the wildness of the terrace makes it one of the best on the island.

Hotel Casal d'Artà
Carrer Rafael Blanes 19, Artà; www.baudot1926.com; €€
A good budget option, this friendly townhouse at the top of town is a delight. Typical island decor goes well with a laid-back vibe, while a sunny dining room and terrace make breakfast a time to linger. The roof is a wonderful place to end the day with a glass of wine. Breakfast is included.

Cases de Son Barbassa
Carretera Cala Mesquida s/n, Capdepera; www.sonbarbassa.com; €€€

Terrace and pool at La Residencia

coloured building offers comfortable accommodation with bright contemporary furnishings. The Mediterranean restaurant has a lovely terrace and the first-floor cocktail bar has occasional live music.

Es Trenc and the South

Hostal Colonial

Ingeniero Gabriel Roca 9, Colònia de Sant Jordi; www.hotel-colonial.es/en/; €

A straightforward but pleasing little place in a quiet little town, this *hostal* is big on family seaside appeal, with its own ice-cream parlour and a huge range of hot chocolate. Very competitive prices. Breakfast included.

S'Hotelet de Santanyí

Plaça Major 23, Santanyí; www.hoteletsantanyi.com; €€€€

This smartly renovated townhouse is a welcome addition to Santanyí's hip village scene. Crisp white linen against honey-coloured stone makes for soothing weekends away, while the lively central plaza location gives a sense of being at the heart of things.

Felanitx to Petra

Sa Bassa Rotja

Finca Son Orell, Camí Sa Pedrera s/n, Porreres; www.sabassarotja.com; €€€

A thirteenth-century country mansion set in large grounds, with sports facilities, a spa and a restaurant using locally produced ingredients, plus live music on Saturday nights

and a barbecue on Sundays. Rooms are furnished in contemporary Mallorcan style. It's ideal for a relaxing or active short break.

Son Bernadinet

Carretera Campos–Porreres Km 5.9; www.son-bernadinet.com; €€€

A lovely manor house with minimalist decor, surrounded by almond orchards, with its own vegetable gardens, and a log fire to warm you in winter. It feels miles from anywhere, but it's only 15 minutes' drive to the nearest beach.

León de Sineu

Carrer dels Bous 129, Sineu; http://leondesineu.com; €€

An elegant, antique-furnished hotel with large airy rooms, close to the central square in this attractive old town. There's a welcoming atmosphere and a good restaurant, Sa Boveda, which serves Mallorcan cuisine and has a wide selection of wines. The pool is in a shady garden.

Wine Country

Virrey Finca Hotel

Carretera Inca-Sencelles Km 2.4, www.virreyhotel.com/en/; €€€

This old privateer's mansion has been turned into a comfortable country-house hotel where mod cons meet traditional furnishings. There is also an on-site restaurant, serving delicious Mallorcan cuisine, and a swimming pool.

Restaurants

When it comes to eating out in Mallorca there's plenty of diversity, though certain areas are much stronger than others. As in most cities, Palma has something to suit a range of tastes and budgets, but once you get outside urban areas it helps to know what you are doing. The restaurants selected follow, roughly, the routes outlined in the walks and tours, but in some cases it's worth travelling a bit further to eat well. You eat much better on the southeast coast than the northeast, and it is worth making the detour if food is the main purpose of your trip.

Opening hours, especially in rural areas and depending on the season, can be a bit erratic. If you want to be sure, it pays to check the appropriate website or sometimes call in advance.

Eating out is no longer particularly cheap, though there are some bargains to be had.

Palma

13%
Carrer Sant Feliu 13a; www.13porciento.com; €–€€
Just off Passeig des Born, this attractive wine bar serves excellent salads and plates of ham and cheese as well as fish and meat courses and an excellent variety of wine by the glass or bottle. Good-priced tapas menu for two (or more).

Marc Fosh Restaurant

La Bóveda
Carrer Botería 3; tel: 971 714 863; www.facebook.com/labovedapalma/; €
This iconic Palma tapas bar is the place to go to rub shoulders with local people and tuck into plates of maple-sweet *jamón Ibérico*, slabs of Manchego cheese, *pimientos de padrón* (sweet, and occasionally spicy fried green peppers) and heaps of local seafood. Sit at the bar or on the terrace and enjoy with an ice-cold *caña* (small draught beer) or a glass of the local wine.

El Bungalow
Carrer Esculls 2, Ciutat Jardí; tel: 971 262 738; €€€
Ask any chef in Mallorca their favourite fish restaurant and at least half of them will come back with this place. Little more than a stone shack on the beach, it serves fish just the way it should be: fresh and simply grilled – and it's just 15 minutes from central Palma, out in the direction of the airport.

Caballito del Mar
Passeig de Sagrera 5;
http://caballitodemar.info; €€
The place to go for fish and shellfish cooked to suit your requirements. There's an outside terrace just around the corner from lively Plaça Sa Llotja but it's separated from the waterfront by the busy main road. The paellas and *frituras* are always popular.

Celler Pagès
C/Felip Bauza 2, off c/Estanc;
www.cellerpages.com; €€
Small, intimate and well-established restaurant in a pleasantly decorated, two-room basement with a family atmosphere and a rustic feel. They serve traditional Mallorcan food – try the stuffed marrows with home-made mayonnaise on the side, the delicious roast leg of duck with dried plums and grilled vegetables or the tongue with capers.

Celler Sa Premsa
Plaça Bisbe Berenguer de Palou 8;
www.cellersapremsa.com; €€
This is a real institution, which has been operating for 60 years. Great ambience and good, filling, everyday Mallorcan classics. Competitive prices too.

Ca'n Eduardo
C/Contramoll Mollet s/n;
http://caneduardo.com; €€
On the top floor of a plain, three-storey block overlooking the city's fishing harbour, this large and modern restaurant offers a simply superb range of fish dishes – try, for example, the hake in a pea sauce.

Marc Fosh Restaurant
Carrer Missió 7a; http://marcfosh.com; €€€€
Marc Fosh is one of Mallorca's most talented chefs. A staunch proponent of local produce, his fresh take on traditional recipes – like rice with *sobrasada* (the local pork sausage generously laced with paprika) – ensures intensely satisfying eating, and his flagship restaurant is just the place to try it. Check out one of his other two branches: Fosh Lab (Carrer d'En Morei 5; tel: 971 595 301), and Fosh Kitchen (Carrer d'Orfila 4; tel: 971 721 354).

La Mujer De Verde
Plaça Porta de Santa Catalina 1;
www.lamujerdeverde.com; €
This vegetarian restaurant draws a crowd for its set-price lunch menu. The food is inventive and healthy, ranging from wholemeal bread with home-made soups to more substantial pasta and bean dishes. The atmosphere is convivial thanks to lots of longstanding regulars.

Safrà 21
Carrer Illa de Corfú 21, Ciudad Jardin;
www.safra21.com; €€
At lunchtime this restaurant specialises in serving traditional rice dishes; in the evening it becomes Mallorca's first 'Bistronomic' restaurant, focusing on top-quality cuisine at reasonable prices.

St. Ambros Ristorante e Pizzeria

Plaça d'En Coll; www.st-ambros.com; €

There's the *Sant Ambros* café on one side of this little square, the trattoria on the other. The trattoria menu covers all the Italian classics, and although the food isn't fantastic, it is inexpensive, and the portions are substantial. Plaça Coll, on the edge of the Sa Gerrería neighbourhood, is a great place to savour the city.

Andratx to Banyalbufar

Alfresco

Asociación Cultural Sa Taronja, Carrer Andalucía 23, Andratx; www.ccandratx.eu; €€

Something of a well-kept secret, this place works for all seasons. Lushly planted gardens are magical in the summer, while the cosy, fire-lit dining room is a boon in winter months. Live music is staged throughout the year, along with wine-tastings and other cultural events, and the food is superb, much of it home-grown and organic

Son Tomás

Carrer Baronia, 17, Banyalbufar; tel: 971 618 149; €€€

This region isn't particularly strong when it comes to dining, but Son Tomás has enjoyed a sterling reputation since the mid-1980s for its sturdy Mediterranean cooking. It buzzes with atmosphere, and the fish soup, paellas and *fideus* are all firm favourites. Harder-to-please customers insist that the views are better than the food.

Seafood paella

Villages of the Tramuntana

Ca Na Toneta

Carrer Horitzó 21, Caimari; www.canatoneta.com; €€€

Like a little dolls' house, Ca Na Toneta and its creators, Maria and Teresa Solivellas, ooze charm. The delightful dining room makes a fitting backdrop for dishes made from organic products that they grow themselves. They serve a six-course tasting menu, which changes weekly to reflect the nuances of the seasons. It's one worth travelling for. See website for opening days and times.

Dalt Muntanya

Carretera Bunyola–Orient Km 10; www.dalt-muntanya.com; €€€

Part of a hotel of the same name, this restaurant has a fabulous terrace from which to take in the scenery over a hale and hearty menu of hikers' favourites. Plenty of vegetable-rich starters, but the stars are slowly roasted leg of lamb or suckling pig: both superb.

Traffic at Can Xim

Plaça de la Vila 8, Alaró; www.canxim.com; €€€

Don't be fooled by the slightly stressful-sounding name, this is a charmer, with its ancient wood beams and rustic decor – just the sort of place to hole up for a long, lazy winter lunch. The food tends towards the heavy, but features tasty combinations like monkfish and eggplant, and stewed rabbit with confit onions.

Valldemossa to Lluc

Sa Fonda de Lluc
Plaça dels Peregrins 1, Lluc;
www.lluc.net; €€

This vast dining room of austere stone columns and flagstones was the pilgrims' canteen, and it has a certain monastic austerity. It's a good place for dinner at the end of a long day, to enjoy their speciality – wild mountain goat with jugs of lusty red wine.

El Olivo
Carrer Son Canals s/n, Deià;
www.belmond.com; €€€€

La Residencia's fine-dining restaurant draws legions of fans who can't afford a night at the hotel, but can treat themselves to a taste of the high life in elegant and refined surroundings. The modern Mallorcan tasting menu changes seasonally and is one of the best on the island. A slightly cheaper option for lunch and dinner is Café Miró, also at La Residencia, decorated with a unique collection of paintings by the Catalan genius.

Es Port
Port de Valldemossa s/n, Valldemossa;
tel: 971 616 194; www.facebook.com/
restauranteesportdevalldemossa; €€€

A comely restaurant spread over two floors with a pretty terrace looking back over the village and down towards the sea. The food is solid and unfussy, involving seaside classics like paella, steamed mussels, and interesting salads.

Sebastián
Carrer Felipe Bauzá s/n, Deià;
www.restaurantesebastian.com; €€€

An excellent choice for a special night out if your budget doesn't quite reach the dizzying heights of El Olivo. The warm, candlelit ambience and cleverly constructed dishes, such as slow-baked lamb with honey, are just right for a romantic evening.

Xelini
Carrer Archiduque Luis Salvador 19, Deià;
www.xelinideia.com; €€

One of the more low-key eateries in Deià, this lively little tapas bar (previously called El Barrigon) on a pretty terrace has been going strong for many years and draws locals and visitors alike for its unfussy fare. Try the smoked ham, aubergines stuffed with goat's cheese and their speciality of *mar i muntanya* (chicken and prawns). Xelini has served many famous faces, including Catherine Zeta-Jones, Michael Douglas and Susan Sarandon.

Sóller and Port of Sóller

Bens d'Avall
Urb Costa Deià, Ctra Sóller–Deià;
www.bensdavall.com; €€€

About halfway between Sóller and Deià, this gourmet restaurant with a lovely terrace overlooking the sea specialises in New Balearic Cuisine (*nouvelle* cuisine made with local produce). Try the steamed fish with seasonal veg drizzled with herb *vinaigrette*.

Es Canyís
Passeig de Sa Platja d'en Repic 21; http://escanyis.es; €€
Bright and cheerful bistro-style restaurant offering an excellent and extensive range of Spanish dishes from its bayside premises behind the Platja d'en Repic. The snails are a house speciality, but the paella is also tempting, as is the chicken breast in almond sauce.

Sa Cova
Plaça Constitució 7, Sóller; tel: 971 633 222; €€
Pleasant traditional restaurant with some tables on the main square. It serves good *conejo* (rabbit), which appears on many menus in the area, and seafood stew – *cazuela*. They also do a great vegetarian paella.

Kingfisher
San Ramon de Penyafort 25; http://kingfishersoller.com; €€€
Outstanding restaurant, the best in the resort, with a small but extremely well-chosen menu featuring the likes of black seafood spaghetti or mussels and shrimp pasta in squid ink. In an old-ish stone house at the back of the harbour and with a pleasant terrace. Reservations recommended.

Lua
Carrer Santa Catalina 1, Port de Sóller; https://restaurantelua.eatbu.com/; €€
A pretty little restaurant in the Santa Caterina fishermen's district, with a more inventive take on the region's fish produce than most. Spread over two floors, the nicest place to sit is on the narrow terrace with views over the port. Enjoy tucking into local orange salad followed by a succulent fillet of John Dory slathered with *salsa verde*.

Luna 36
C/Lluna 36; http://luna36.es; €€
In a narrow-fronted old building that was once a chocolate factory, this excellent restaurant is arguably Sóller's best. Kitted out in an attractive and modern rustic style and with a small garden terrace, the *Luna* offers a creative range of tapas as well as Mediterranean/Spanish food: the fish of the day is particularly recommended.

Petit Celler Cas Carreter
C/Cetre 4; http://cascarreter.com; €
Long-established, family-run restaurant in a cleverly recycled old wheelwright's workshop – the large and conspicuous wine-barrel bottoms were added later. Offers a mixture of well-presented Spanish and Mallorcan dishes (try the snails) with mains very competitively priced.

La Vila Restaurante
Plaça Constitució 14; https://lavilahotel.com; €€€
A bit of a mixed bag of a place, but one of Sóller's most distinctive restaurants, occupying the ground floor of a handsome *Modernista* building, now a hotel, and complete with vintage - albeit somewhat gloomy - furnishings

El Olivo restaurant, at La Residencia

and fittings as well as a more cheerful and very leafy patio. There are two menus – one for snacks, the other a full restaurant menu featuring both Italian and Spanish dishes – try, for example, the swordfish with leeks. Patchy service – take something to read, just in case.

Pollença and Formentor
La Font del Gall
Carrer Montesió 4, Plaça Almoina, Pollença; tel: 971 530 396; €€

Owned by a Scottish family, the Font del Gall, behind Plaça Major, serves a good range of dishes in a friendly atmosphere, indoors or out on a terrace. There is a good selection of vegetarian options on the menu such as caramelised red onion and goat's cheese tart.

Il Giardino
Plaça Major 11, Pollença; www.ilgiardino.es; €€

This family-run trattoria on the square makes a great place to sit and watch the world go by at night, when it's at its most convivial. Wood-fire cooked pizzas and home-made pastas are excellent. Next door, their shop sells French and Mallorcan cakes and chocolates. Closed Mon.

Stay
Moll Nou s/n, Port de Pollença; www.stayrestaurant.com; €€

A smart restaurant right in the centre of the port that has been operating for years. Fish is the first choice but there are imaginative meat dishes too, including lamb and pigeon ravioli. Caramelised walnut ice cream with green tea *coulis* is a popular dessert. Open every day of the year.

Bay of Alcúdia
Aqua
Port d'Alcúdia; www.aquaalcudia.com; €€

Funky Mediterranean-Asian restaurant and sushi bar with a chill-out terrace overlooking the sea. Live music and DJs in the summer months.

Bistró de Jardín
Corner of Carrer Diana and Carrer Triton, Port d'Alcúdia; www.bistrodeljardin.com/; €€

Value-for-money Mediterranean dishes. Try tuna *tartar* to start followed by the house hamburger and red fruit soup with yoghurt foam for dessert. There is also a gastrobar (€) here serving tapas and sandwiches.

Ca'n Costa
Carrer Sant Vinçens 14, Alcúdia; www.cancostaalcudia.com; €€€

This family-run restaurant in the oldest house in town (1594) has a lovely shady terrace out the back. Specialities include cod with garlic and honey, rabbit with onion and prawns and paellas – there's even a vegetarian one. Friendly staff and excellent service ensure a good experience.

Satyricon
Plaça Constitució 4, Alcúdia; tel: 971 544 997, www.facebook.com/Restaurante.Satyricon/; €€

Housed in the grand surroundings of the old cinema in the main square, this place is perfect for romantic dinners and people watching, especially if you are seated on the balcony. The décor recalls Ancient Rome but the food is decidedly modern market cuisine. Desserts include flambéed strawberries with Amaretto and pineapple soup with spices and coconut cream.

Trattoria Don Vito
Carretera Alcúdia–Artà 11, Port d'Alcúdia; www.don-vito.com; €€
A handy standby for pizza and pasta at the end of the day, offering a solid range of Italian classics as well as more sophisticated dishes such as vitello tonnato and osso buco.

Artà and Cala Torta
Finca Es Serral
Carretera Cala Torta Km 5, Artà; http://fincaesserral.com/Restaurante-Es-Serral; €€
It's a delight to know that restaurants like this still exist: Es Serral is the very heart and soul of a true farm restaurant. All the fruit and vegetables are grown on the owner's plot, the meat reared locally and the food home-cooked. Reserve well in advance to secure a table (and opening hours can be erratic, especially out of season), but it is well worth the forward planning.

La Fragua
Carrer des Pla den Cosset 3, Capdepera; www.lafragua.eatbu.com; €€
Should you make it into Capdepera, a stroll around the ancient battlements of the fourteenth-century castle should help you work up an appetite, which can be sated at La Fragua, which serves traditional Mallorquín dishes with an international twist on a romantic roof terrace.

Caves and Grottoes of the East
La Bodeguita
Avinguda América 14, Cala Ratjada; tel: 971 819 062; www.labodeguita.es; €
La Bodeguita does bargain-priced tapas and hearty main courses. Expect fairly basic service and food that is filling rather than award-winning, but it has pretty views over the seafront and is good for something cheap and cheerful.

Sa Llotja
Carrer Pescadores s/n, Porto Colom; www.restaurantsallotjaportocolom.com; €€€
A smart fish restaurant in the port of this little town, Sa Llotja is raised up above the beach on a glassed-in first floor. It has fantastic views, which can be especially dramatic in stormy weather – it's open year-round – and offers a solid repertoire of locally caught, simply cooked fish and seafood. A three-course menu de la semana (weekly menu) with wine and coffee is served for lunch and dinner.

Roland
Carrer de la Tramuntana 11, Porto Cristo; http://roland-restaurant.es/en/; €€€€
Founder and head chef Roland Schulte offers a regularly changing menu using seasonal ingredients and fresh fish sourced from local fisheries. There's no sea view but the food more than makes up for it.

A beautifully presented plate at Marc Fosh Restaurant

Es Trenc and the South

Restaurant Es Port
Carrer Virgen del Carmen 88, Cala
Figuera; tel: 971 165 140; €€

A jolly, family-run place that's big on
crowd-pleasing classics ranging from
tapas and sangria, grilled fish and man-
sized steaks, stuffed aubergines and
grilled vegetable salads, through to
home-made pizza and pasta. It's a sweet
location, too, with wonderful views
over the port. Booking is essential.

Sal de Coco
Moll de Pescadors, Colonia de Sant
Jordi; tel: 971 655 225; €€€

Run by a young female chef and her sisters,
this modern restaurant is named after
the local salt. House specials include fish
from La Cabrera, home-made pastas such
as spinach and prawn ravioli with curry
sauce and Idiazabal cheese with quince
for dessert. There is a good wine list too.

Felanitx to Petra

Es Brot
Carrer Ràpita 44, Campos; tel: 653 751 528; €€€

Often described as the best traditional
restaurant in Mallorca, Es Brot's diverse
menu of classics like pork-stuffed
cabbage leaves, pickled partridge and
sturdy rice dishes is excellent. Be sure
to come with a healthy appetite.

Es Celler de Petra
Carrer de l'Hospital 46, Petra; tel: 971 561 056; €€

Huge and cavernous restaurant
serving heaped plates of traditional
food, including meat roasted in
a traditional wood oven.

Son Bascos
Carretera Palma-Manacor, Km 29,
Montuiri; tel: 626 94 68 60; €

Set on a quail farm, the speciality of
this traditional Mallorcan restaurant is,
of course, quail. Try quails' eggs with
garlic mayonnaise to start followed by
grilled quail with salad. Don't panic if
you don't fancy quail – there are other
dishes on offer, including options for
vegetarians. The home-made desserts
include carrot and almond cake.

Wine Country

Can Jan
Plaça de l'Església 5, Binissalem;
www.canjan.es; €€

An informal and relaxed restaurant
located on the main square of Binissalem,
serving popular dishes such as paella,
octopus croquettes and Bolognese.
Children's menu also available.

Celler Can Ripoll
Carrer Jaume Armengol 4, Inca;
www.restaurantcanripoll.com; €€

Opened in 1768, this cellar restaurant was
used mainly by local workers as a place
to fill their wine jugs. Food wasn't offered
until the 1940s, the speciality being a fairly
hardcore *frito mallorquín* – stir-fried offal.
These days you can also find excellent but
rather more pedestrian stuffed cabbage
leaves and roast suckling pig. The daily
menu (weekdays only) is a real bargain.

Nightlife

If you're looking for frenetic nightlife, Mallorca probably isn't the island for you, although things can get lively in Palma in the summer. Once outside the city you will find a much slower pace of life, especially when you hit rural areas and some of the quieter coastal towns and villages. If you're staying in Estellencs (tour 4), for example, the most you can hope for is a beer in the village bar, although tourist resorts tend to be livelier. For that reason, the bulk of the listings here concentrate on what's happening in Palma, with a sprinkling of recommended places elsewhere.

Palma

Ábaco

Carrer Sant Joan 1; www.bar-abaco.es

No visit to Palma is complete without stopping at this legendary cocktail bar. Famed for its over-the-top decor, and gigantic fruit and floral arrangements, there's nowhere quite like it for your gin and tonic.

Auditorium

Passeig Marítim 18; www.auditoriumpalma.com

Home to the Ciutat de Palma Symphony Orchestra and a host of cultural events throughout the year, ranging from contemporary dance to opera. Check out what's on ahead of your trip; tickets can be hard to come by.

Casino de Mallorca

Porto Pi Centro; www.casinodemallorca.com

The island's only casino can be fun. It's a fairly upmarket place once you get away from the slot machines, and provides a good excuse to get dressed up and indulge in an *Ocean's Eleven*-style fantasy.

Cine Ciutat

Carrer Emperatrix Eugenia 6; www.cineciutat.org

The only original-language cinema in town, Cine Ciutat shows a fair number of independent films as well as the blockbusters. Auditoriums are small and cosy, giving it an art-house feel.

Cuba Bar and Restaurant

Carrer de Sant Magí 1, Palma Centre & Marina; www.hotelhostalcuba.com/es

Housed in a beautiful colonial building in the trendy Santa Catalina district of Palma, this popular hotel, café, bar and club features wicker chairs and leafy palms in the ground floor café and a rooftop Sky Bar offering great sunset views over Palma. There is also a restaurant serving Mediterranean dishes. Downstairs is where the DJ's spin their tunes until the small hours.

Cocktails at sunset

Made in Brasil
Passeig Marítim 27; tel: 670 372 390

If you seek samba, salsa and other snake-hipped Latin rhythms, this is where to head; the place sizzles until 4am most nights of the week, attracting some serious dancers.

Puro Beach
Cala Estancia s/n (airport exit); www.purobeach.com

The first of a growing number of swanky beach clubs to pepper the coast, Puro is the full-time haunt of the island's oh-so beautiful crowd in summer. It opens early for sunbathing by the pool, yoga sessions and champagne brunches, segueing effortlessly into a more clubby vibe once the sun goes down.

The luxurious Puro Beach

Virtual Club Balneario Illetas
Passeig Illetes 52, Illetes; www.balnearioilletas.com

This resort's second beach club – after Puro – Balneario is a little less achingly trendy and offers a more relaxed vibe. Like Puro, you can spend the day lounging by the sea, have lunch, then let your sundowner lead you gently into the evening.

Outside Palma

Nikki Beach
Avinguda Notario Alemany 1, Magaluf; www.mallorca.nikkibeach.com

One of the latest offerings from the chain of exclusive beach clubs with branches in St Tropez, St Barts, Dubai, Ibiza and Miami. What started as a beach café has grown into a luxury beachclub brand. Here you can relax on a sunbed by day and party by night. Excellent restaurant serving dishes inspired by the place. Closed in winter.

Pirates
Carretera Sa Porrassa 12, Magaluf; www.piratesadventure.com

The show at Pirates has been running since the early 1980s and is wildly popular. Book well in advance and treat the whole family to what may be the best 'espectaculo' this side of Broadway.

Essentials

Accessible travel

If travelling with a wheelchair, inform the airline or ferry service in advance. Assistance should be on hand for getting through arrival and departure halls. Not all bars, restaurants or hotels are equipped with ramps or lifts – far from it – so check the facilities in advance if you can. Amongst the several companies specializing in accessible travel, one port of call is Enable Holidays (www.enableholidays.com/mallorca).

Age restrictions

The age of consent in Spain is 16. You can smoke and drink from 18. To drive a car or motorbike over 125cc you need to be 18.

Budgeting

Mallorca has become more expensive in recent years as the island has moved upmarket. All prices below are approximate and given only as a guide.

Getting there

Air fares vary enormously. Flights from the UK with a budget airline can range from around £60 return in off-season to £300 or more in high season. To compare prices and find the best deals, head to www.skyscanner.net.

Accommodation

Hotels can be more expensive than on the Spanish mainland. Rates for two sharing a double room during high season can range from as low as €100 in a *hostal* to as much as €500 at a top-of-the-range hotel. A comfortable, pleasant three-star hotel will cost about €100–€150. Rates drop considerably out of season.

Meals

Where it's available, the *menú del día*, a fixed price midday meal, is usually an excellent bargain, costing around €15–25 for a reasonably good three-course meal with one drink included. In a bar, a continental breakfast (fresh orange juice, coffee and croissant) will cost around €10–15; a coffee €5. The average price of a three-course à la carte meal, including house wine, will be about €45 per person. You can pay considerably less, but at top restaurants you may pay more than twice that much. The price of wine has increased: you will pay about €3–€5 for a glass of wine in a smartish bar.

Attractions

Most museums and galleries charge an entry fee of around €10. Entry to La Real Cartuja, Valldemossa costs €15; the Coves

Flying the EU flag

del Drach around €18. Water parks are more expensive, around €30 (children €20). A two-hour trip in a glass-bottomed boat costs around €25 (children half-price).

Ferries
Inter-island ferries between Mallorca and Menorca are reasonable for foot passengers (about €50 return), but quite expensive if you take a car – about €250 for a vehicle and two passengers. The ferry from Mallorca to Ibiza is about the same price. Deals are often available, especially if you book well in advance.

Useful prices
A *caña* (small draught beer): €3.00
Glass of house wine: €3–5
Main course: budget restaurant €12, mid-range €18, expensive €25+
Hotels: budget €100, moderate €150, luxury €200+
Taxi from Palma airport to city centre: €35
A single bus ticket: €5

Children

Most Spaniards adore kids. Even fairly late at night, you will find that restaurants welcome little ones with open arms, and most serve child-friendly meals. Nearly all sights and theme parks offer a discount for under-12s, and resort hotels are generally pretty good when it comes to children's activities.

Autumn sunrise in the interior of the island

Climate

Mid-June until September is virtually rainless, with wall-to-wall sunshine. In July, the hottest month, temperatures usually range from 30°C (86°F) in the afternoon to about 20°C (68°F) at night, although 2024 saw record-breaking highs of 40 degrees. Autumn temperatures are typically around 24°C (75°F), but there are often short heavy rains in early September; October is the wettest month. April and May see a little rain with lots of sunshine and moderate temperatures. In winter, expect some rain and cool winds, but most days are sunny, and it is usually warm enough at midday to sit outside. Average maximum/

Parc del Mar, Palma

Numerous beaches are family-friendly

Christmas in Palma de Mallorca

minimum winter temperatures are 15°C (59°F) and 7°C (45°F).

Clothing

Mallorca is pretty low-key, though older people dress up a bit for their evening *paseo* (promenade); a T-shirt and shorts are the minimum requirement for both men and women. Never wear beach gear in towns (you can now be fined for this), and when visiting churches cover your shoulders and knees. Going topless on the beaches is fairly normal, though total nudity should be kept to designated beaches.

In spring and autumn bring lots of light layers and a mac. In summer you won't need much

Pristine paintwork

more than something to cover up with, but bring something warm and waterproof in the winter.

Crime and safety

Mallorca is generally pretty safe and serious crime extremely rare. Employ the same precautions you would anywhere, though: keep your eye on belongings, especially in crowded areas, and take care when withdrawing money from ATMs. Leave extra valuables in the hotel safe; make a photocopy of your passport and carry it with you. If you hire a car, don't leave property visible inside.

If any of your property is lost or stolen you must report it to the police within 24 hours if you intend to make a claim on your insurance policy.

Customs

EU nationals may purchase up to 800 cigarettes, 200 cigars or 1kg tobacco, 10l of spirits and 90l of wine. Non-EU nationals may purchase 200 cigarettes, 50 cigars, 250g loose tobacco, 1l spirits and 2l wine.

Electricity

220 volts AC. British appliances work perfectly well but need an adaptor, as sockets are the two round-pin type; US appliances need a transformer.

Embassies and consulates

Australia: in Madrid; www.spain.embassy.gov.au.

Canada: in Madrid;
www.international.gc.ca.
Ireland: in Madrid; www.ireland.
ie/en/spain/madrid/.
UK: Carrer Convent dels Caputxins
4, Edificio Orisba B, Palma; tel:
933 66 62 00; www.gov.uk.
US: Edificio Reina Constanza, Carrer
Porto Pi 8, 9th floor, Palma; tel: 971
403 707; www.usembassy.gov.

Emergencies

Police, fire, ambulance: 112

Festivals

Most towns and villages have a local
festival celebrating their patron
saint, which incorporates abundant
dancing, eating and drinking. The
most interesting have appearances
by *cavallets* – dancers with cardboard
hobby-horses strapped to them
– and *dimoni* – red-clad devils.
Highlights include: Palma's carnival
in February; Semana Santa (Holy
Week) in Pollença; Moros y Cristianos
(Christians and Moors) in Sóller on
8–10 May; festivals of classical music
in Pollença and Deià throughout
July and August; Festa des Vermar
(Wine Festival) on the last Sunday
of September in Binissalem. Check
www.illesbalears.travel/en/ for a
comprehensive list of events.

Green issues

Mallorca has invested heavily
in developing 'slow tourism' by
expanding hiking trails, bicycle routes
and *agroturismos* (rural hotels and
restaurants) which often grow their
own produce. The tourist 'eco tax'
introduced in 2016 aims to promote
responsible development and tourism.
In March 2021, the Balearic Islands
introduced a ban on single-use plastics
within the hospitality sector and in
supermarkets to reduce the amount
of plastic found in the sea, which
is a major issue for this region.

Health

Vaccinations
None currently required.

Health care and insurance
EU/EEA citizens are eligible for free
treatment in state-run hospitals. UK
visitors should obtain a UK Global
Health Insurance Card (GHIC)
online (www.nhs.uk/ghic). Visitors
from the US will need private health
insurance, and it is strongly advised
that all travellers take out private
medical and travel insurance.

Pharmacies and hospitals
For accidents and emergencies, go
to Hospital Son Espases, Carretera
de Valldemossa 79; tel: 871 205
000, www.hospitalsonespases.
es, where some staff also speak
English and German.
   Most towns and villages have first-
aid stations or doctor's surgeries: the

Potential purchases in Pollença

Casa de Socorro or *Cruz (Creu) Roja.* There are pharmacies *(farmacias)* on most main streets in Palma (look out for the green cross), and in all major towns. In most towns an effective system of rotation operates whereby there is always one chemist open round-the-clock in each area. A posted sign in front of each should indicate which chemists are on duty that night, and which is closest to where you are. Some pharmacies, such as Farmacia Balanguera (www.farmaciabalanguera.com), are open 24 hours. *Farmacias* are amply stocked with over-the-counter remedies, and many drugs can be purchased without prescription; however, your particular medication may not be available, and they do not honour foreign prescriptions, so bring with you any prescription medicine you require.

Medical emergencies

If you have a medical emergency while in Spain, your hotel should be able to recommend reliable professionals who speak several languages. The local embassy or consulate will also have a list of English-speaking doctors. You can also go to the local hospital emergency department or medical clinic to receive treatment on presentation of a UK Global Health Insurance Card. If no help is near at hand, call the medical emergency number: 112.

Hours and holidays

Hours still revolve around the long lunchtime siesta, though that is slowly changing. Shop hours are 9.30am–1.30pm and 4.30–8pm. Museums generally open 9am–6pm (although smaller ones may keep the siesta).

Banks are only open in the mornings from 9.30am–2pm, Monday to Friday, but some open on Saturday in winter. Restaurants serve lunch from 1.30–3.30pm. In the evening local people usually eat between 9 and 11pm.

Internet

Practically the whole of Palma is covered with free Wi-fi. The island's authorities plan to extend the free coverage beyond the city limits, but the process is a lengthy one and there are still many areas without a reliable Wi-fi connection.

LGBTQ+ travellers

There's not a massive scene in Mallorca and most of it is concentrated in Palma, but citizens are generally indifferent, and you shouldn't encounter any problems. There are quite a few lively clubs and bars in the old town. See www.mallorcagayguide.com and www.benamics.com.

Lost property

There are lost property departments at the airport on the ground floor and at Palma's Town Hall. It is also worth

Mallorca's winding roads are perfect for cycling

checking with the police station nearest to where you lost your belongings.

Maps

Free tourist maps of Palma are given out at most hotels and the tourist office, likewise in bigger towns like Sóller. In rural areas maps are useful for getting your bearings, but not very reliable for route planning.

Media

Print media

Most UK and German papers arrive daily in Palma and the main resorts, along with the *International Herald Tribune, Wall Street Journal* and *USA Today*. The English-language *Majorca Daily Bulletin* (www.majorcadaily bulletin.com) gives local and UK news and entertainment listings. Local publication the *Diario de Mallorca* (www.diariodemallorca. es) is good for up-to-the-minute information on what's on, and all the Spanish national newspapers and magazines are widely available.

Television

Most hotels and bars have television, broadcasting in Castilian, Catalan and Mallorquín. All but the smallest of hotels generally have satellite channels (predominantly German, but also French, channels along with the ubiquitous English-language Sky, BBC, CNN, etc.).

Ambulance in Palma

Money

Currency

The euro has been the Spanish monetary unit since 2002.

Credit cards

Major international credit cards such as Visa, Eurocard and Mastercard are widely accepted, but smaller businesses sometimes prefer cash. American Express is only accepted in some places.

Cash machines

Credit and debit cards are useful for obtaining cash from ATMs – cash machines – which are found in all towns and resorts.

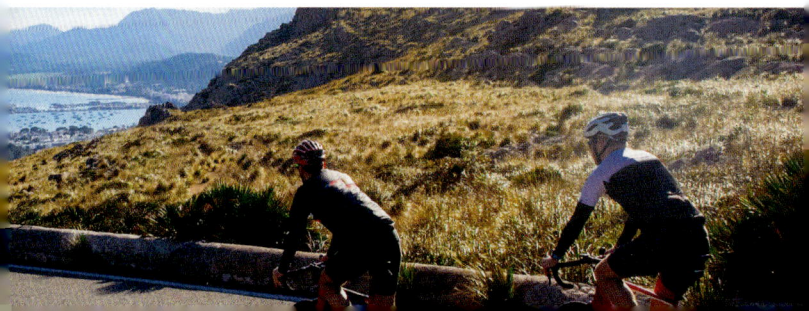

Tipping

In some restaurants service is already included (look for *servicio incluído* on the bill). Otherwise, tips range from rounding up to the nearest euro at a bar, to 10 percent in a smart restaurant.

Taxes

Spain applies a standard rate of VAT (IVA) of 21 percent on most goods and services, including hotels; 10 percent is charged on foodstuffs and in restaurants. The 2016 tourist tax adds up to €4 to the daily rate of accommodation.

Reclaiming VAT

In order to be eligible, as a tourist, for a refund of the Spanish IVA (Value Added Tax), you must come from a non-EU country. Tell the shop concerned that you intend to reclaim the VAT, which is currently 21 percent in Spain. Since 2018, there has been no minimum purchase amount required for this refund. You will be given a form which you must get stamped at a duty reduction office at the airport before departure. Go to the desk of one of the companies authorised to give you a tax refund. If you leave the country other than by air, get the customs post to validate your form and then take a copy back to the shop you bought the goods from and it will make the refund. The process is explained at www.globalblue.com.

Police

In an emergency dial 112.

There are three types of police, distinguishable by their uniforms: in black and white are the Policía Nacional, who are in charge of most things. The Policía Municipal (Local or Metropolitan) are responsible for traffic control, while the Guardia Civil, still dressed in traditional dark-green uniforms, have jurisdiction only in rural areas.

Post

Palma's main post office is at Carrer Constitució 6 and is open Monday to Friday 8.30am–8.30pm and is closed on weekends. Many other post offices on the island (all recognisable by a yellow and white sign and the words *Correos y Telégrafos*) are only open 8.30am–2.30pm. Post boxes are yellow.

Stamps can also be bought at tobacconists *(estancos)*, which are easily identifiable by their maroon and yellow *Tabacos* sign over the door.

Public holidays

As in all Catholic countries, local saints' days may be celebrated as holidays, but only the days of the major saints (see the list opposite) are public holidays throughout the island.
1 Jan: New Year's Day (Año Nuevo/Any Nou)

Botanicactus botanical garden

6 Jan: Epiphany (Reyes Magos/Reis Mags)
19 Mar: St Joseph (San José/Sant Josep)
Good Friday (Viernes Santo/ Divendres Sant)
1 May: Labour Day (Dia del Trabajo/Treball)
Ninth Thursday after Easter: Corpus Christi
24 June: St John (San Juan/Sant Joan)
29 June: St Peter and Paul (San Pedro y San Pablo/Sant Pere i Sant Pau)
25 July: St James (Santiago/ Sant Jaume)
15 Aug: Day of the Assumption (Asunción/Assumpció)
12 Oct: Spanish National Day (Dia de la Hispanidad/Hispanitat)
1 Nov: All Saints (Todos los Santos/Tots Sants)
6 Dec: Constitution Day (Dia de la Constitución/Constitució)
8 Dec: Immaculate Conception (Inmaculada Concepión/Concepció)
Christmas Day (Navidad/Nadal)

Religion

The official religion of Mallorca is Catholicism, though the majority of locals are fairly lax about it. Many attend mass at Christmas and Easter, when it can be quite festive.

Smoking

As of 1 January 2011, smoking has been banned in public places across Spain.

Cala Mesquida

Telephones

The international code for Spain is 34. To call within Spain, you must always dial the area code (971 for the Balearics), then the number, even when phoning within the same town. To make an international call, dial 00 for an international line plus the country code plus the phone number, omitting any initial zero where there is one. Calls are cheaper after 10pm on weekdays, after 2pm on Saturday, and all day Sunday.

Mobile phones. Most UK mobile phones can be used in the Balearics. Contact your service provider if you are unsure, and it's a good idea to find out about any money-saving tips such as buying bundles of minutes. It is cheaper to receive calls than to make them. If you are going to make lots of calls within Spain it is worth buying a Spanish SIM card, eSIM (digital SIM card) or maybe even a new phone from a phone shop. Well-known networks are Movistar (www.movistar. es), Orange (www.orange.es) and Vodafone (www.vodafone.es).

Time zone

Spain is on Central European Time, one hour ahead of Greenwich Mean Time. When it is noon in London, it is 1pm in Mallorca.

Toilets

Toilets *(serveis/servicios)* are generally clean and well kept, but public

Sunset over the coast

toilets are few and far between. If you duck into a bar you should buy something, as most are for patrons only. In Palma, head for a department store such as El Corte Inglés. *Dones/damas* stands for ladies, *cavallers/caballeros* for gentlemen.

Tourist information

Tourist information is readily available in most parts of Mallorca, although many offices close in winter. The following list is not comprehensive.

Local tourist offices
Palma: Plaça de la Reina 2, tel: 971173 990; Passeig del Born 27, tel: 902 102 365; Plaça d'Espanya, tel: 902 102 365; Plaça de les Meravelles, Platja de Palma, tel: 902 102 365.
Airport: tel: 971 789 556.
Alcúdia: Passeig Pere Ventanyol s/n, www.alcudiamallorca.com.
Colònia Sant Jordi: Gabriel Roca s/n, tel: 971 656 073 (closed Nov–Mar)
Pollença: Guillem Cifre de Colonya s/n, www.pollensa.com.
Port d'Alcúdia: Passeig Marítím s/n, www.alcudiamallorca.com.
Port de Pollença: Passeig Saralegui s/n, www.pollensa.com.
Port de Sóller: Canonge Oliver 10, www.ajsoller.net/ca.
Sóller: Plaça d'Espanya 15, www.ajsoller.net/ca.
Valldemossa: Avinguda de Palma 7, www.ajvalldemossa.net/ca.

Tourist offices abroad
Spanish embassies and consulates are listed on www.exteriores.gob.es/en. **Information on Spain in English** is brought together on www.spain.info/en.

Tours

Local tourist offices will have details of guided bus and walking tours in the area but here is a selection of more interesting ones:
Cooltra: Carrer Monsenyor Palmer 3, Palma, www.cooltra.com. Small group tours around Palma by scooter.
Mallorca Hiking: www.mallorcahiking.com. A wide range of guided walks for all levels including strenuous hikes, gastronomy and architecture.
Mallorca Wine Tours: www.mallorcawinetours.com. Tours of Mallorca's vineyards on a small tourist train.
Palma City Sightseeing: www.city-sightseeing-spain.com/es/palma-de-mallorca. Open-top bus tours of Palma.
Tramuntana Tours: www.tramuntanatours.com. Walking, mountain biking and sea-kayaking in small groups.

Transport

Airports and arrival
Palma de Mallorca's huge **Son Sant Joan airport** (PMI; www.aena.es)

Quad bikes for hire in Magaluf

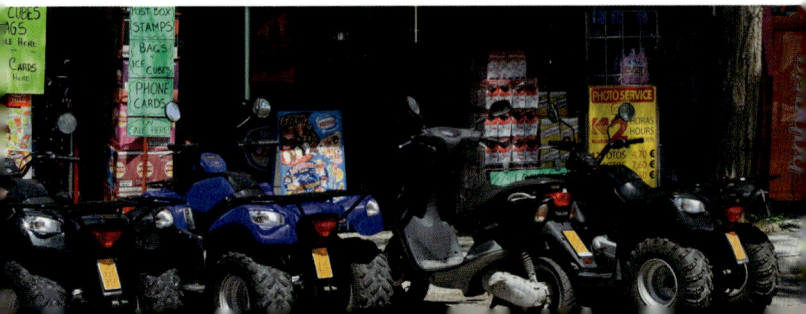

is linked by regular non-stop flights from London, Dublin, Berlin and Frankfurt, with frequent flights from many other European cities. Flights from the US and Canada also go via London airports and Barcelona or Madrid. Numerous budget airlines fly to Palma from airports all over the UK.

The airport is about 11km from the city centre. There are buses every 20 minutes (journey time about 30 minutes). Bus No. 1 runs to Plaça d'Espanya, and to the port with stops en route (check the website for bus times; www.palmademallorcaairport. co.uk). Taxis are readily available (journey time about 15–20 minutes) and fares are reasonable.

Bus in Valldemossa

Arriving by boat
Car ferries operate daily from Barcelona and Valencia to Palma. The slower, overnight trip takes 8 hours on Trasmediterránea (www.armas trasmediterranea.com/en); during peak holiday season, it also operates a faster ferry, which takes 4.5 hours. Baleària operates a fast ferry from Barcelona to Alcúdia, which takes 5.5 hours (www.balearia.com).

Public transport
Buses
There are several bus companies in Mallorca, travelling to virtually every point on the island. In Palma, most services begin at the Plaça d'Espanya or

the bus station close by– see www.tib. org for details. City buses are also efficient. There is a set fare for city journeys, and you buy your ticket on the bus. A Palma bus schedule detailing city routes from Empresa Municipal de Transports (EMT) is available on www.emtpalma.cat.
Metro
Palma's metro system is the fifth in Spain and consists of two lines (M1, M2) with nine stations each. M1 connects Estació Intermodal on Plaza d'Espanya with the university, while M2 links Plaça d'Espanya with Marratxí.

Cycle route along the seafront

Trains

As well as the famous old train, which runs seven times a day (five in winter) between Palma and Sóller, there is a train from Palma's Plaça d'Espanya to Inca which runs on to Sa Pobla and Manacor. Primarily a commuter train, it leaves both the island capital and Inca about once every hour, with extra trains at rush hour, stopping at Santa Maria del Camí, Consell and Binissalem along the way. For Sóller trains check out www.trendesoller.com; for Inca and Manacor trains, see www.tib.org or ask at the station.

Taxis

Palma has several taxi ranks, and cabs can be hailed on the street. All have meters and are reasonably priced, though you pay extra for luggage and trips to and from the airport. Trips across the island, however, are quite expensive. Official prices are posted at cab ranks, and drivers also carry a list (theoretically).

Driving in Mallorca

Rules and regulations

Drive on the right. Seat belts are compulsory for front and back seats. Children under 12 must be seated in a special car seat or booster seat depending on age/height. Don't drink and drive: the permitted blood-alcohol level is low and penalties are strict. Compulsory equipment includes a spare tyre, a warning triangle and a reflective jacket.

Road conditions

Generally good, although many are narrow, and mountain routes have numerous hairpin bends and can get very busy in the summer. The motorway that loops around to the north of Palma (connecting the airport with points west of the city), is known as the *Via Cintura* and is signposted as such.

Speed limits

Motorways 120kmph (74mph), two-lane highways 100kmph (62mph), other main roads 90kmph (55mph), built-up areas 50kmph (31mph), unless otherwise indicated.

Parking

In Palma this can be difficult. Your best bet is to head for one of the city centre underground car parks (for instance opposite the cathedral at the Parc de la Mar). Parking fines are steep, and as it is more difficult to collect fines from tourists, there is a tendency to tow away hire cars.

Car hire

This is relatively inexpensive, and all the major international agencies are represented. In high season, book well in advance and remember that local companies often set a minimum rental of three or four days. Always check what's included: third-party insurance is, by law, but fully comprehensive is usually extra and it is advisable to have it. You need to be 21 to hire a car and must have a full driving licence and a credit card.

Marina at Andratx

EVs in Mallorca

Distances in Mallorca are relatively small, which has helped boost the use of EV vehicles. All the major car rental companies now offer EV vehicles at competitive rates – indeed, their cheapest vehicles are often electric. Furthermore, each municipality has installed free EV charging points with 350 stations now in place and the number growing every year. The whole system is applied island-wide by MELIB (Mobilitat Elèctrica a les Illes Balears) with the MELIB App showing station location points and their status in real time.

Bicycle and scooter hire

A practical and enjoyable way to see the island is to hire a bicycle, and this can be done in most resorts – hotels and tourist offices have leaflets. Mopeds and scooters are also available, but you'll need a special licence. Prices vary widely, so shop around. Remember that a helmet is compulsory when riding a motorcycle, whatever the engine size. Ask for a helmet and for a pump and puncture kit, in case you get stuck with a flat tyre, and always carry ID. In Palma, go to Palma on bike, Avinguda Gabriel Roca 15, tel: 971 918 988, www.palmaonbike.com. Pro Cycle Hire will deliver your bike direct to your resort hotel if arranged in advance; tel: 971 866 857 or check www.procyclehire.com. It also organises daily ride-outs (meeting point in front of the shop at Carrer Corb Mari 6, Puerto Pollença).

Visas and passports

British citizens can stay in Spain for 90 days within any 180-day period with a valid passport. Visitors from EU/EEA countries may enter with a valid national identity card or valid passport. US citizens, Australians and New Zealanders require a valid passport and are automatically authorised for a three-month stay.

Websites

Useful websites are peppered throughout the book, but the following are good for general information: www.seemallorca.com: for tips on what's on and where to go. www.mallorca.es/en/inici: the official tourism portals for the island. www.palma.es: Palma city council's site. www.spain.info/en/: Spain's official tourism website with useful information on the Balearic Islands.

Weights and measures

Mallorca uses the metric system.

Women travellers

Women travelling alone should find Mallorca an easy-going, non-threatening place to explore. As anywhere, avoid walking home late at night alone.

Hiring a car is the easiest way to explore the island

Language

Mallorca's language is Mallorquín, a dialect of Catalan. During Franco's dictatorship, the teaching and publication of Catalan was banned, and replaced by Spanish/Castilian (Castellano), although people still spoke the language at home. With the arrival of regional autonomy in 1978, Catalan/Mallorquín was re-established, and has become a symbol of Mallorcan identity, although almost everyone also speaks Spanish.

As a result of this, maps and street signs (should) use Catalan exclusively. That said, most words are fairly similar between the two languages, though some are completely dissimilar. Signs indicating various points of touristic or other interest are almost always in Catalan. Throughout this book, we have tried to give the Catalan version of the place name, and the words and phrases below are also in the official local language.

Useful words and phrases

General
yes *sí*
no *no*
please *si us plau*
thank you (very much) *(moltes) gràcies*
you're welcome *de res*
excuse me *perdoni*
hello *hola*

good morning *bon dia*
good afternoon *bona tarda*
good evening/night *bona nit*
goodbye *adéu*
How much is it? *Quant val?*
What is your name? *Com es diu?*
OK *d'acord*
My name is… *Em dic…*
Do you speak English? *Parla anglès?*
I am English/American *Sóc anglès (anglesa)/americà/ana*
I don't understand *No ho entenc*
Please speak more slowly *Parli més a poc a poc, sisplau*
Can you help me? *Em pot ajudar?*
I'm looking for… *Estic buscant…*
Where is…? *On és…?*
I'm sorry *Ho sento*
I don't know *No ho sé*
When? *Quan?*
What time is it? *Quina hora és?*
left *esquerra*
right *dreta*
straight on *tot recte*
opposite *al davant*
beside *al costat*

On arrival
I want to get off at… *Voldria baixar a…*
Is there a bus to…? *Hi ha un autobús cap a…?*
Which line do I take for…? *Quina línia agafo per…?*
airport *l'aeroport*
railway station *l'estació de tren*

Sample Mallorca's signature pastries

bus station *l'estació d'autobusos*
bus *l'autobús*
platform *l'andana*
ticket *un bitllet*
return ticket *un bitllet*
de anada i tornada
toilets *els lavabos/serveis*

Emergencies
Help! *Auxili!*
Stop! *Pari!*
I am sick *Em trobo malament*
I have lost my passport/wallet
He perdut el passaport/la cartera

Shopping
I'd like to buy… *Voldria comprar…*
How much is it? *Quant val?*
Do you take credit cards?
Es pot pagar amb targeta?
I'm just looking *Estic mirant*
receipt *el tiquet*
chemist *la farmàcia*
bakery *el forn de pa*
book shop *la llibreria*
department store *els grans magatzems*
grocery *el botiga de queviures*
tobacconist *l'estanc*
market *el mercat*
supermarket *el supermercat*

Sightseeing
tourist information office
oficina de turisme
free *gratuït*
open *obert*
closed *tancat*
every day *tots els dias*

Dining out
breakfast *l'esmorzar*
lunch *el dinar*
dinner *el sopar*
meal *el menjar*
set menu *el menú del dia*
drink included *beguda inclosa*
wine list *la carta de vins*
red wine *vi negre*
white wine *vi blanc*
the bill *el compte*
glass *la copa* (for wine),
el vas (for water)
I am a vegetarian *Sóc vegetarià/ana*
I'd like to order *Voldria demanar*
tax included *IVA inclòs*

Days of the week
Monday *Dilluns*
Tuesday *Dimarts*
Wednesday *Dimecres*
Thursday *Dijous*
Friday *Divendres*
Saturday *Dissabte*
Sunday *Diumenge*

Social media
Are you on Facebook/X?
Que tens Facebook/X?
What's your user name?
Quin és el teu nom d'usuari?
I'll add you as a friend.
T'agregaré com a amic.
I'll follow you on X.
Et seguiré a X.
Are you following…? *Segueixes…?*
I'll tag you in the pictures.
T'etiquetaré a les fotos.

Conversing in Palma, next to a headless street artist

Books and film

Until fairly recently, Mallorca has been largely ignored by the worlds of literature and film. However, over the past decade humorous expat memoirs à la Peter Mayle and Chris Stewart have been published and the island is increasingly used as a film location – multi-million-pound investments have created two state-of-the-art studios.

Here is a selection of the best English-language books and movies. For further information about local books visit Fine Books, Carrer Morey 7, in Palma, and for the latest film news see www.imdb.com.

Books

General background
Mallorca: The Making of the Landscape by Richard Buswell. An interesting read about the island's history.
Tuning up at Dawn by Tomàs Graves. Robert Graves's son writes about life and music.
Wild Olives by William Graves. Robert Graves's other son's account of growing up in Deià.
Miró by Janis Mink. This beautifully illustrated book tracks through the artist's life and times.
Franco: A Biography by Paul Preston. A penetrating – and monumental – biography of Franco and his regime, which provides as clear a picture as any of how he won the Civil War and survived in power so long.

Walking, climbing and birdwatching
Landscapes of Mallorca by Valerie Crespi-Green. A companion for walkers and hikers.
Finding Birds in Mallorca by Dave Gosney. Shows the best sites to see Mallorca's birdlife.

Food
Bread and Oil by Tomàs Graves. An insider's look at two of Mallorca's great products.

Travel accounts
A Woman Unknown: Voices from a Spanish Life by Lucia Graves. This moving memoir, by Robert Graves's daughter, is a succinct and thoughtful exploration of a life in between cultures – English and Mallorcan/Spanish. No one has better explored the deadening psychological weight of Franco's regime.
Snowball Oranges by Peter Kerr. The first of several entertaining books about a Scottish expat settling into life on the island.
A Lizard in my Luggage by Anna

Library at Real Cartuja (Royal Carthusain monastery) de Valldemossa

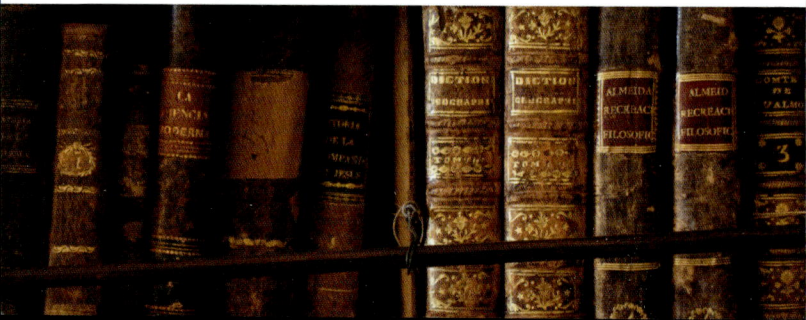

Nicholas. The first of several enjoyable books by a London PR consultant who moves to the Sóller Valley.

A Winter in Majorca by George Sand. Sand's scathing account of her stay on the island in 1838–9 with Chopin.

A House in the High Hills: Dreams and Disasters of Life in a Spanish Farmhouse by Selina Scott. The former TV newsreader's humorous account of renovating her property in the Serra de Tramuntana.

Fiction

The Mallorca Connection by Peter Kerr. The first of several comedic crime novels featuring fictional Scottish detective Bob Burns.

Rafael's Wings by Sian Mackay. A Scottish ornithologist finds herself in a mysterious world when she goes to work in the Mallorcan mountains.

The Bloody Bokhara by George Scott. Mallorcan murder mystery set in the now-closed Scott's Hotel in Binissalem.

Film and TV

Our Girl Friday (1953). British comedy starring Joan Collins about a woman who is shipwrecked on a desert island with three men.

The 7th Voyage of Sinbad (1958). Some of the scenes from this much-loved fantasy film with special effects by Ray Harryhausen were shot in the Coves d'Artà.

Evil Under the Sun (1982). Several locations in Mallorca including Sa Dragonera and Formentor were used for this star-studded interpretation of Agatha Christie's book.

Presence of Mind (1999). Filmed on the Raixa Estate and starring Harvey Keitel and Sadie Frost, this film is a chilling adaptation of *The Turn of the Screw* by Henry James.

Four Last Songs (2006). *Downton Abbey*'s Hugh Bonneville leads an international cast in this British romantic comedy with a musical theme.

Cloud Atlas (2013). Sa Calobra, Sóller and Formentor are the real stars of this adaptation of David Mitchell's best-selling book which explores how history repeats itself.

The Stranger Within (2013). A dark psychological thriller in which a psychiatrist and his wife, played by William Baldwin and Estella Warren, encounter murder and mayhem on a Mediterranean island.

A Long Way Down (2014). Pierce Brosnan and Toni Collette star in this comedy, based on the novel by Nick Hornby, about four people who form a surrogate family to help each other through tough times.

The Night Manager (2016). A popular BBC miniseries based on John le Carré's novel, starring Tom Hiddleston and Hugh Laurie, featuring some stunning Mallorcan landscapes.

Frédéric Chopin and George Sand Museum

About this book

CREDITS

The Rough Guides Walks & Tours series helps you discover the world's most exciting destinations through our expert-curated trip plans: a range of walks and tours designed to suit all budgets, interests and trip lengths. These walks, driving tours and site excursions cover the destination's most quintessential attractions as well as a range of lesser-known sights, while food and drink stops for refreshments en route are highlighted in boxes. If you're not sure which walk to pick, our Best walks & tours for... feature suggests which ones work best for particular interests. The introduction provides a destination overview, while the directory supports the walks and tours with all the essential information you need, as well as our pick of where to stay while you are there and select restaurant listings, to complement the more low-key options given in the trip plans.

About the authors

This edition of Rough Guide Walks and Tours Mallorca was updated by Phil Lee, building on work by Victoria Trott and Tara Stevens. Victoria Trott has updated several guidebooks on the Spanish mainland and Balearic Isles and has travelled extensively in the country. Tara Stevens writes about Spanish lifestyle, food and wine for a wide variety of international publications.

Help us update

We've gone to a lot of effort to ensure that this edition of the **Rough Guides Walks & Tours Mallorca** is accurate and up-to-date. However, things change – places get "discovered", new gems open up, restaurants and rooms raise prices or lower standards. If you feel we've got it wrong or left something out, we'd like to know, and if you can remember the address, the website, whether or not it was free to enter – so much the better.

Please send your comments with the subject line "**Rough Guides Walks & Tours Mallorca Update**" to mail@uk.roughguides.com. We'll acknowledge all contributions and send a copy of the next edition (or any other Rough Guide if you prefer) for the very best emails.

Credits

Rough Guides Walks & Tours Mallorca

Editor: Lizzie Horrocks

Author: Phil Lee

Picture Editor: Piotr Kala

Picture Manager: Tom Smyth

Cartography: Katie Bennett

Layout: Grzegorz Madejak

Production Operations Manager: Katie Bennett

Publishing Technology Manager: Rebeka Davies

Head of Publishing: Sarah Clark

Photo credits: All images Shutterstock except: Belmond La Residencia 90/91, 92/93; Bodegas Angel 82, 82/83, 83R; Fotolia 72T; Four Seasons Resorts 91T; Greg Gladman/Apa Publications 6TL, 7CL, 11, 12/13, 13R, 14, 16, 19, 22, 24, 25R, 35, 36, 36/37, 37R, 40/41, 41R, 42, 44, 46, 46/47, 47R, 48, 48/49, 49R, 56, 56/57, 57R, 60, 60/61, 61R, 77R, 78, 79, 104, 106, 107, 110, 112, 114, 115, 116, 117, 118; Hotel Bon Sol 86/87; iStockphoto 18, 52T, 54/55; Jumeirah Port Soller 96/97; Leonardo 98/99; MNAC 27; Palacio Ca Sa Galesa 88T; Puro Group 87T, 103T; Simply Fosh 94/95; Son Brull 92T

Cover credits: The Soller train **Shutterstock**

Printed in Czech Republic

This book was produced using **Typefi** automated publishing software.

First Edition 2025

Distribution

UK, Ireland and Europe

Apa Publications (UK) Ltd

sales@roughguides.com

United States and Canada

Ingram Publisher Services

ips@ingramcontent.com

Australia and New Zealand

Booktopia

retailer@booktopia.com.au

Worldwide

Apa Publications (UK) Ltd

sales@roughguides.com

Special Sales, Content Licensing and CoPublishing

Rough Guides can be purchased in bulk quantities at discounted prices. We can create special editions, personalised jackets and corporate imprints tailored to your needs.

sales@roughguides.com

http://roughguides.com

Index

MAP LEGEND

- ● Start of tour
- → Tour & route direction
- ❶ Recommended sight
- ❶ Recommended restaurant/café
- ★ Place of interest
- ❶ Tourist information
- ⚊ Statue/monument
- ✉ Main post office
- 🚌 Main bus station
- 🌾 Windmill
- 🏰 Castle / ruin

- Park
- Important building
- Hotel
- Transport hub
- Shop / market
- Pedestrian area
- Urban area